Rural Women Workers in India's Unorganized Sector

RURAL WOMEN WORKERS
in
India's Unorganized Sector

By

DR. MEENU AGRAWAL

Associate Professor and Head,
Department of Economics,
Ginni Devi Modi Girls (Post-graduate) College,
Modinagar

New Century Publications
New Delhi, India

NEW CENTURY PUBLICATIONS
4800/24, Bharat Ram Road,
Ansari Road, Daryaganj,
New Delhi – 110 002 (India)

Tel.: 011-2324 7798, 4358 7398, 6539 6605
Fax: 011-4101 7798
E-mail: indiatax@vsnl.com • info@newcenturypublications.com
www.newcenturypublications.com

Editorial office:
LG–7, Aakarshan Bhawan,
4754-57/23, Ansari Road, Daryaganj,
New Delhi – 110 002

Tel.: 011-4356 0919

First Published: **July 2012**

ISBN: **978-81-7708-328-6**

Published by New Century Publications and printed at Salasar Imaging Systems, New Delhi.

Designs: Patch Creative Unit, New Delhi.

PRINTED IN INDIA

About the Book

Census 2011 estimated India's population at 121 crore. Rural population accounted for 68.8 percent (83.3 crore) of the total population. A very large proportion of rural population is —either wholly or significantly—dependant on agriculture and allied activities like horticulture, animal husbandry and fisheries.

According to the final report of the National Commission for Enterprises in the Unorganised Sector (NCEUS) [Chairman: Arjun Sengupta] released in April 2009, workers in the unorganized (or informal) sector constitute more than 93 percent of the total workforce of India. Unorganized sector workers are those who do not have any job security, income security or social security and are therefore extremely vulnerable to exogenous shocks.

Women in rural areas are clearly the overwhelming proportion of the workforce in the informal rural economy and most of them suffer from various forms of insecurities and vulnerabilities.

The present work explains and examines the conditions of rural women workers. It also focuses on policies and programmes of the Government to ameliorate their socio-economic existence.

Author's Profile

Dr. Meenu Agrawal is Associate Professor and Head, Department of Economics, GDM Girls (Post-graduate) College, Modinagar. She obtained her Ph.D. degree from Ch. Charan Singh University, Meerut in 1991. She specialises in the areas of rural development, poverty alleviation, and women empowerment. With more than 27 years of teaching experience and 20 years of research experience, she has authored 2 books and co-authored 3 books in areas of her specialisation.

Dr. Agrawal has published 52 research papers in journals/magazines of repute. She has also contributed and presented papers at national and international seminars. She is Director of a Major Research Project sponsored by University Grants Commission (UGC), New Delhi and Indian Institute of Public Administration (IIPA), New Delhi.

Contents

Preface

Women workers in India have always been active contributors to the national income. Their contributions, however, have rarely been acknowledged, thus far. An important characteristic of the Indian female work force is that most of it is employed in the unorganised sector, currently estimated to be 94 percent of the total women workers.

Women are not recognised as workers and even though they put in long hours of work, the returns are very low. They have limited access to tools and equipment; innovations in communications and technology almost completely bypass them. They face multiple entry barriers into the mainstream markets, use of social protection is restricted and inclusion in policy dialogue–labour or economic–is very low.

It is well-known that the women all over the world are part and parcel of the labour market. But it is also true those women everywhere are excluded from crucial economic activities. For example, in the agricultural sector in India, women are employed in production, processing and preservation of agricultural produce, but are not much active in plugging. In both rural and urban areas they are engaged in work which sometimes has either no exchange value or very low exchange value. The inferior status and poor facilities offered to them vis-à-vis males accentuates further their poor economic condition and pushes them into the unorganized sector.

Like almost all other societies of the world, the Indian society is also dominated by men. Since the ancient period, the women are treated as subordinate to men. Our Hindu texts have fully described the position of women in the society.

The status of women has been explained by 'Manu' in the following words; "Duteous girl obeys her father, husband sways the duteous wife, son controls the widowed mother, never free a woman life."

In India, the working women generally work in

unorganised sector. National Commission on Self-employed Women (2006) has recorded that of the total women workers about 94 percent are in unorganised sector, whereas only 6 percent of them are in organised sector. Thus, it can be emphatically remarked that unorganised or informal sector in India is the women sector.

Though there is no attraction in unorganised sector, yet women seek employment in this sector because of ignorance, illiteracy, easy entry and exit, lack of skills, less waiting period and irregular nature of employment. Moreover, the poverty and economic necessity have also put women in this sector. These women mostly belong to scheduled caste, scheduled tribes, other backward classes and economically weaker sections of the society. Poor women in poor families accept any forms of employment at whatever wages without considering the nature of jobs. It is, therefore, clear that the increasing cost of living has compelled the poor women to go for such jobs. They feel the burdens of family expenditure and therefore, share this responsibility with their husbands.

The role of women in Indian society is vital. The future of children depends by and large upon the mother. The women in poor societies perform the dual function as they take care of children at home and also go out of home to perform their duties of employment. By virtue of set up of the society in India, women workers perform all domestic responsibilities at their homes. Besides work in informal sectors, they look after their domestic problems, do cooking, washing, cleaning, bringing water from outside taps on wells and other household chores before going for work and also after coming back from work. As these chores are considered to be their pious duty, they get no help from their male counterparts. Males consider these duties as below their dignity.

The informal sector provides jobs of local nature. It involves the local people around women, therefore, concentrate in this sector. Women in informal sectors are employed in construction work, brick-kiln work, small-scale and cottage industries, mine works, trade, transport and communication works, agricultural works and in services etc. In informal sector category, self-employed women are also included. They work in jobs such as Knitting, sewing and weaving, selling household commodities, fresh vegetables and fruits etc. The women also get employment in the domestic work as servants and sweepers in urban areas.

After the Industrial Revolution, women entered the labour market to seek employment in various jobs. In India, the women started their economic role after Independence but their participation still remains unrecognized. The informal sector in India provides employment to a vast majority of women in agriculture, industrial establishments, construction and building works and in domestic services. The self-employed women are also included in informal sector. Though the women are exploited in this sector, yet they continue in it because of economic necessities and other compulsion. Illiteracy, ignorance, lack of skills and the irregular nature of employment have made this sector suitable for them. In this sector, the hours of work are long, jobs are unsecured, there is no limit for minimum wages and wages are paid to them discriminately, minimum facilities at workplace are not provided and they face ill treatment, exploitation and sexual harassment. The government has taken steps to solve the problems of women workers in this sector but much success has not been achieved.

The status of women in informal sector is very much disadvantageous, as they do not get enough pay to improve the quality of their lives. In both rural and urban areas they are not offered fair wages and satisfactory terms and conditions of work. Sometimes, they are employed in works which have no exchangc valuc or very low exchange value. In informal sector, the method of payment of wages, retrenchment, sanction of leave etc. are all arbitrary. The hours of work of these workers are longer than permitted by the law. Moreover, there is no overtime payment to them. They are also not provided medical and maternity benefits. A glaring drawback of this sector is that laws cannot be implemented in it forcefully. Summarily, the informal sector gives to women only insecure and unprotected employment with meagre wages, long hours of work and unhygienic conditions of work. They get no ideas and information regarding hygiene, nutrition and diseases. It is worth mentioning here that there is hardly any opportunity to improve their earnings so that short and long-term decisions may be taken for more efforts and training for necessary skills among women workers for their improvement and upliftment.

It is painful to mention that women in informal sector have ad-hoc or temporary jobs with no provision of social security, welfare measures and rewards. Thus, their socio-economic condition, in general is miserable.

Undoubtedly, the Constitution of India has made strong provisions to safeguard the interest of women in the field of economic activity but these provisions are not adhered to in the real practice. It is a fact that women are paid much less in comparison to men for doing the same work and they are discriminated in entering into gainful employment. They are also not given the opportunity to avail the benefits of vocational training and formal education. Further, they are exploited by the money-lenders and middlemen etc. In reality, there is no economic independence to women. There are almost no women unions in informal sector and therefore, their cause or grievance is not represented.

Though the women in informal sector in India work under inhuman and deplorable conditions yet their participation in this sector will remain for long. The yearly increase in population and the small number absorbed by the formal sector clearly indicate that the informal sector will grow overtime. It has been estimated that over 60 percent of employment in Nairobi, 50 percent in Djakanta and 45 percent in Kolkata, Mumbai and Ahmedabad are in informal sector. It has been observed that due to certain socio-institutional compulsions many women do not prefer whole time employment. Moreover, women employment in informal sector is rising due to various other reasons such as with the adoption of Structural Adjustment Programme.

Women are losing their grounds in formal sector of the economy, the fall in incomes of households due to law level performance of the economy is also leading to increased entry of women into the informal sector, the process of globalisation, liberalisation and export-oriented industrialisation are also leading to increase in women workers in the informal sector of the country's economy. Thus, the informal sector has become an integral part of our economy and if it is withdrawn suddenly, the whole uneconomic system will collapse. It is true that the existence of informal sector largely depends on the continued relative advantage that the formal sector obtains by linking its activities with informal sector.

Women play a very crucial role in socio-economic development of a country. As a matter of fact, the prosperity of a nation by and large depends upon the status and development of its women. However, the question of women welfare has lately attracted the attention of sociologists, economists and research scholars. The report of National Commission on Labour (1969) has admitted that "there is a large element of unprotected labour working in different parts of the country particularly in some parts of towns and cities. Very little is known about it and much less has been done to ameliorate its condition of work."

Women labour is an important factor of production. It has been seen that women have moved parallel with men in almost all walks of life but their condition in informal sector has not improved. It is a well known fact that informal sector is the backbone of Indian workforce. It holds a very important place in Indian economy. The informal sector is also viewed as an integral part of the competitive economy. It provides readymade jobs to the people. Thus, it helps in removing seasonal unemployment.

In view of the sizeable employment opportunities in the informal sector and its capacity to provide a wide variety of goods and services, the condition of women engaged in this sector has to be studied in greater detail.

Women are considered as inferior agents of production though a large number of them are concentrated in informal sector. The U.N. Report 1975 has stated that "two thirds of the world's quantitative work is done by women. In return they receive mere 10 percent of all incomes and own only 1 percent of all means of production. This reveals in many ways and at many levels that women remain relatively powerless."

"In India some of the vital aspects of women's employment in the informal sector are totally neglected in research. Most studies have been carried out in Metropolitan cities and there is hardly any study on the pattern and problems of informal sector in smaller cities and towns." Thus, very little has come to be known about the region wise or area wise aspects of functioning of informal sector and more specifically of the condition of women labour in this sector. So an empirical study of a particular area or region can be more useful in improving the conditions of women in this sector. A micro-level study will enable proper analysis of the problems of women in informal sector. To reduce poverty in this sector, it is necessary to know a lot about these women area-wise. Thus, any plan to improve working women conditions will require the knowledge of every aspect of their economic and social life.

I take this opportunity to express my deep sense of gratitude to the President, Manager and all the Members of The Management Committee, Ginni Devi Modi Girls Post-graduate College, Modinagar, for their valuable support and guidance. I am also grateful to the Principal, Professor Rita Bakshi for being a constant source of inspiration.

My family members, particularly my mother-in-law, Shrimati Gaura Devi, my brothers-in-law Shri Satish

Aggarwala, Supreme Court Advocate, Dr. Adish Aggarwala, Additional Advocate General (Tamil Nadu and Punjab), sisters-in-law, Shrimati Shashi Agarwal and Shrimati Madhu Garg have played the central role in facilitating my studies.

My greatest debt is to my mother Shrimati Kusum Lata, for providing me psychological support and encouragement during the course of the study. I am very lucky to receive precious guidance and immense co-operation in my daunting task from my father Dr. R.C. Agrawal, Principal, Ex-Dean, Faculty of Commerce and Business Administration, CCS University, Meerut.

It is a matter of great pleasure and pride for me to express my deepest sense of gratitude and indebtedness to my husband Shri Sudhish Aggarwala, Senior Manager, IOC R&D Centre, Faridabad under whose inspiring guidance this work has been completed.

I am grateful for the unparallel help given by my sister Dr. Babita Agrawal, Associate Professor in Economics, Arya Kanya Post-graduate college, Hapur and brother Dr. Pawan Agrawal at various stages in the preparation of this work. Finally, I express my affection for my sons Nitish Aggarwala and Kavish Aggarwala for their moral support and cheerfulness.

June 2012 **MEENU AGRAWAL**
Modinagar

1

Unorganized Sector and Women

1.1 Unorganized Sector Defined

The term unorganised sector was first used by Hart in 1971 who described the unorganised sector as that part of urban labour force, which falls outside the organized labour market. In the unorganised sector, work situations are not in official record and working conditions are not protected by law. So the problems of female workers in unorganised sector are not properly known. It has been pointed out by Hart that one of the major problems is that their working conditions are worst.

That optimistic vision of economic transition did not match what was actually happening in the world. In the late 1960s and 1970s, a large section of the population in the developing countries was suffering from poverty and working outside the organized sector in activities that were later broadly termed as "unorganized". Due to population growth and urban migration, the active labour force was growing at a much faster rate than the availability of jobs in the organized sector. The focus of development policies was gradually shifting from pure economic growth to growth with equity and the eradication of poverty. Interest was, thus, generated in sectors outside the organized economy that was providing a livelihood to a large section of the poor. Hence, the concept of the unorganised sector was born. In defining the unorganised sector, self-employed with or without family labour and micro-enterprises with less than five workers, are also included.

In analysing the contribution of the unorganised sector, emphasis is placed on the pervasive importance of the link between organised and unorganised activities that are not confined to particular occupations or even economic activities.

Unorganised sector in India is broadly characterized as consisting of units engaged in the production of goods and services with the primary objectives of generating employment and incomes to the persons concerned. For statistical purpose, the unorganised sector is regarded as a group of production units, which form part of the household sector as household enterprises or equivalently, unincorporated enterprises owned by households.

In India, the term unorganised sector has not been used in the official statistics or in the National Accounts Statistics (NAS). The terms used in the Indian NAS are 'organised' and 'unorganised' sectors. The organised sector comprises enterprises for which the statistics are available from the budget documents or reports etc. On the other hand, the unorganised sector refers to those enterprises whose activities or collection of data is not regulated under any legal provision or do not maintain any regular accounts. In the unorganised sector, in addition to the unincorporated proprieties or partnership enterprises or, enterprises run by cooperative societies, trust, private and limited companies are also covered. The unorganised sector can therefore, be considered as a subset of the organised sector.

Like almost all other societies of the World, the Indian society is also dominated by men. Since the ancient period, the women are treated as subordinate to men. Our Hindu texts have fully described the position of women in the society.

1.2 Status of Women in India

Women empowerment is not a new issue in India. Most of our pre-Islamic and pre-Christian African societies were matrilineal. Our women lost their prestige, thanks to Indian and oriental cultural imperialism which gave men the upper hand in our daily affairs. In the unorganised sector, women are still not on top.

Women workers in India have always been active contributors to the national income. Their contributions, however, have rarely been acknowledged, thus far. An important characteristic of the Indian female work force is that most of it is employed in the unorganised or the informal sector, currently estimated to be 78.4 percent of the total women workers. The percentage goes up to 80.7 percent, if women working in the urban areas are also included.

Women are not recognised as workers and even though they put in long hours of work and the returns are very low. They have limited access to tools and equipment; innovations in communications and technology almost completely bypass them. They face multiple entry barriers into the mainstream markets; use of social protection is restricted.

It is well known, that the women all over the world are part and parcel of the labour market. But it is also true that women everywhere are excluded from crucial economic activities. For example, in the agricultural sector in India, women are employed in production, processing and preservation of agricultural products, but are not much active in plugging. In both rural and urban areas they are engaged in work which sometimes has either no exchange value or very low exchange value. The inferior status and poor facilities offered to them vis-à-vis males accentuates further their poor economic condition and pushes them into the unorganized sector. Sometimes because of restrictions put against them they are unable to enter into unorganised sector. In unorganised sector they are employed as domestic servants, sweepers, construction workers, brick-kiln workers, agro industries workers and self employed workers in knitting, sewing and weaving etc. Due to certain economic compulsions these women are pushed to low- productivity jobs.

The time women spend on paid and unpaid work is typically greater than the time men spend in the labour market. Unpaid family work is rarely recorded in official statistics. It manifests itself only indirectly in the labour market in the form of gender differences in labour force participation rates, sector of employment, hours of work, and wage level.

On the whole, labour force participation rates for women are lower than those for men. However, these differences are often exaggerated because the definition of the participation rate fails to capture many aspects of women's work, particularly time spent on childbearing and other household tasks. Men are usually in the labour force throughout the prime working years (age 20-60), and their participation rates are typically more than 90 percent in virtually every country. Female participation rates vary widely across countries. In 1990, for every ten men in the labour force there were two women in the Middle East and North Africa, three in South Asia, six in Sub-Saharan Africa, and seven in Southeast Asia (United Nations, 1991). Worldwide, 41 percent of women of age of 15 years or more are in the labour force, but in developing countries the corresponding figure is 31 percent. These numbers are deceptive; however, because they do not take into account the agricultural work that women do in developing countries of the world.

FAO has noted that while the overall proportion of the economically active population (EAP) working in agriculture declined during the 1990s, the percentage of economically active women working in agriculture at the global level remained nearly 50 percent through 2000, with an even higher percentage in developing countries (61 percent) and in LDCs (79 percent). Furthermore, although FAO projections to 2010 indicate a continued reduction in the overall female participation in agriculture globally, the percentage of economically active women working in agriculture in LDCs is projected to remain above 70 percent.

The female contribution to the overall economy is high throughout Asia and the Pacific region, particularly in terms of labour input into agriculture. Bangladesh, Bhutan, Cambodia, China, India, Myanmar, Nepal, Pakistan and Vietnam have particularly high percentages of women employed in the agricultural sector, with estimates ranging between 60 and 98 percent. Indeed, in most Asian countries the number of women employed in agriculture as a percentage of the EAP is higher than that of men. As FAO reports, "this finding is even more significant given that data for the economically active population in agriculture tends to exclude the unpaid work by rural women in farm and family economies. If unpaid work were included, the figures for female employment in agriculture would be even higher."

1.2.1 Manu on Women: Manu explained the status of women the following words; "Duteous girl obeys her father, husband sways the duteous wife, son controls the widowed mother, never free a woman life."

The society has assigned different fields of activities to men and women. Women have been sheltered as gentle wife, a pious daughter, a virtuous sister and a fertile mother. They have gained respect in the society only in these capacities, undoubtedly, a great social value has been assigned to women in Indian society but many restrictions have been placed on them. They are normally expected to perform their roles in the aforesaid capacities within the four walls of the house.

Mahatma Gandhi believed that "Swaraj would be meaningless without reforms of the social structure and upliftment of the weaker sections namely the women and the lower social strata to a position of equality with others".

He did not compromise himself in the matter of women's rights. However, changes in the thinking and attitude towards women have taken place recently.

Education is the corner stone of women empowerment because it enables them to respond to opportunity to challenge their traditional roles and change their lives. The National Educational Policy of 1986 and National Policy for the, Empowerment of women 2001 clearly laid out that Education must strive towards empowering women. Educating women benefits the whole of society. It has a more significant impact on development than men's education. When women feel they can operate in society on the same terms as men, then we can call women empowered.

The increasing trend of women education has given opportunities to them to enter into various employments but their work is treated as a supplementary and balancing force in the nation's work force, which has made them susceptible in all respects. Thus, in the field of employment, they are exploited physically, socially and economically and they face all sorts of discriminatory treatment. It is a fact that in most of the cases, employers showed no inclination to employ women due to their activities in domestic affairs, restricted mobility, repeated maternity leave and unsuitability especially where physical work is required. Some employers do not want to employ women as they find them insincere, irregular and less productive as compared to men.

In India, the working women generally work in unorganised sector. National Commission on Self-employed Women (1998) has recorded that of the total women workers, about 94 percent are in unorganised sector, whereas only 6 percent of them are in organised sector. Thus, it can be emphatically remarked that unorganised or informal sector in India is the women sector.

Though there is no attraction in unorganised sector, yet women seek employment in this sector because of ignorance, illiteracy, easy entry and exit, lack of skills, less waiting period and irregular nature of employment. Moreover, the poverty and economic necessity have also put women in this sector. These women mostly belong to scheduled castes, scheduled tribes, other backward classes and economically weaker sections of the society. Poor women in poor families accept any forms of employment at whatever wages without considering the nature of jobs. It is, therefore, clear that the increasing cost of living has compelled the poor women to go for such jobs. They feel the burden of family expenditure and therefore, share this responsibility with their husbands.

The role of women in Indian society is vital. The future of children depends by and large upon the mother. The women in poor societies perform the dual function as they take care of children at home and also go out of home to perform their duties of employment. By virtue of set up of the society in India, women workers perform all domestic responsibilities at their homes. Besides work in organised sectors, they look after their domestic problems, do cooking, washing, cleaning, bringing water from outside taps or wells and other household chores before going for work and also after coming back from work. As these chores are considered to be their pious duty, they get no help from their male counterparts. Males consider these duties as below their dignity.

The unorganised sector provides jobs of local nature. It involves the local people around women, therefore, concentrate in this sector. Women in unorganised sectors are employed in construction work, brick-kiln work, small-scale and cottage industries, mine works, trade, transport and communication works, agricultural works and in services etc. In unorganised sector category, self-employed women are also included. They work in jobs such as knitting, sewing and weaving, selling household commodities, fresh vegetables and fruits etc.

The women also get employment in the domestic work as servants and sweepers in urban areas.

Women's role in agriculture received attention in Indian policy circles during the Seventh Five Year Plan. Since then, several programmes for women in agriculture were implemented in India. Some of them are listed below:

1. Special donor-assisted programmes for women in agriculture in selected states.
2. Women Component Plan
3. Initiatives for gender mainstreaming

Besides, the government and NGOs supported rural women in organising themselves and accessing capital and other resources through the following programmes:

1. Rural Livelihood Programmes of the Central and State Rural Development Departments.
2. Micro finance initiatives through women self-help groups

(SHGs).

These initiatives increased the awareness of the role of women in the economy; and improved their access to information, inputs and technologies. In addition, the programmes highlighted the constraints the women face in accessing assets, inputs, credit, knowledge, markets and services. However, the initiatives have several limitations.

The agriculture sector contributes about 32 percent in the Net National Product (NNP). It is worth mentioning that about 70 percent of the total working population and 84 percent of all economically active women are engaged in agriculture. It the agricultural sector in India, women are employed in various agricultural operations such as processing and preservation of agricultural produce, transplanting, weeding, harvesting, hay making and rarely in ploughing. They are also engaged in forestry, fishing, orchard, livestock and allied activities. As a matter of fact, the women perform two thirds of the work in the agriculture sector but still their work is not recognized. Women are one third of the world's official labour force but are concentrated in the lowest paid occupations and are more vulnerable to unemployment.

The unorganised work force in India is estimated 457 million workers nearly 94 percent of total work force. The unorganised workforce is comprised of three main segments. Firstly, unorganised employment in agriculture comprises of self-employment in small-scale farm units and as agricultural labourers, which continue to be important in India, representing 60 percent of total employment. Secondly, employment in unorganized enterprises/sectors outside the agriculture represents another 28 percent of total unorganized employment. Thirdly, unorganized employment outside unorganized enterprises and outside agriculture is estimated 6 percent of total unorganized workforce. Among the total non-agricultural workforce, 133 million workers or 83 percent are in the unorganized economy.

The status of women in unorganized sector is very much

disadvantageous, as they do not get enough pay to improve the quality of their lives. In both rural and urban areas they are not offered fair wages and satisfactory terms and conditions of work. Sometimes, they are employed in works which have no exchange value or very low exchange value. In unorganized sector, the method of payment of wages, retrenchment, sanction of leave etc. are all arbitrary. The hours of work of these workers are longer than permitted by the law. Moreover, there is no overtime payment to them. They are also not provided medical and maternity benefits. A glaring drawback of this sector is that laws cannot be implemented in it forcefully.

Similarly, the unorganized sector gives to women only insecure and unprotected employment with meagre wages, long hours of work and unhygienic conditions of work. They get no ideas and information regarding hygiene, nutrition and diseases. It is worth mentioning here that there is hardly any opportunity to improve their earnings so that short and long-term decisions may be taken for more efforts and training for necessary skills among women workers for their improvement and upliftment.

It is painful to mention that women in unorganized sector have ad-hoc or temporary jobs with no provision of social security, welfare measures and rewards. Thus, their socio-economic condition, in general is miserable.

Though the women in unorganised sector in India work under inhuman and deplorable conditions yet their participation in this sector will remain for long. The yearly increase in population and the small number absorbed by the organised sector clearly indicate that the unorganised sector will grow overtime. It has been estimated that over 60 percent of employment in Nairobi, 50 percent in Djakanta and 45 percent in Kolkata, Mumbai and Ahmedabad are in unorganised sector. It has been observed that due to certain socio-institutional compulsions many women do not prefer whole time employment.

Moreover, women employment in unorganised sector is rising due to various other reasons such as with the adoption of Structural Adjustment Programme women are loosing their grounds in organised sector of the economy. The fall in incomes of households due to low level performance of the economy is also leading to increased entry of women into the unorganised sector, the process of globalisation, liberalisation and export-oriented industrialisation are also leading to increase in women workers in the unorganised sector of the country's economy. Thus, the unorganised sector has become an integral part of our economy and if it is withdrawn suddenly, the whole economic system will collapse. It is true that the existence of unorganised sector largely depends on the continued relative advantage that the organised sector obtains by linking its activities with unorganised sector.

1.3 Constitutional Safeguards for Women

The constitution of India has provided a number of fundamental rights, which grant men and women equal rights, privileges and treatment in the field of economic activity. Article 14 of Indian Constitution says that all citizens are equal in the eyes of law. Article 19 says that every citizen has the right to practice any profession or to carry on any business or occupation. Article 15(1) states that the State shall not discriminate any citizen on grounds of race, caste, religion, sex and place of birth. Article 15(3) empowers the State to frame special provisions for women and children. Article 16(1) states that "there shall be equality of opportunity for all citizens in matters relating to employment. In Article 39, the 'Directive Principles' of State policy state that the State shall in particular direct its policy towards securing:

1. That the citizens, men and women equally have the right to adequate means of livelihood;
2. That there is equal pay for equal work for both men and women;
3. That the health and strength of workers, men and women

and the tender age of children are not abused;

4. That the citizens are not forced by economic necessity to enter professions unsuited to their age and strength.

Moreover, Article 42 directs the states to make provision securing and human conditions of work and to provide maternity relief. Providing for equal rights and opportunities for women and men, the Constitution of India also makes special provisions for women.

Undoubtedly, the Constitution of India has made strong provisions to safeguard the interest of women in the field of economic activity but these provisions are not adhered to in the real practice. It is a fact that women are paid much less in comparison to men for doing the same work and they are discriminated in entering into gainful employment. They are also not given the opportunity to avail the benefits of vocational training and organised education. Further, they are exploited by the money-lenders and middlemen etc. In reality, there is no economic independence to women. There are almost no women unions in unorganised sector and therefore, their cause or grievance is not represented.

2

Review of Literature on Socio-economic Conditions of Women

Before any research project is preceded, it is very pertinent to thoroughly review the relevant literature available on the subject. The researches or studies already done by other investigators should be referred in the research women. It improves and upgrades the research standards, findings and conclusions.

A number of economists, social workers, research scholars and organisations have conducted studies at macro, regional and micro level, related to women workers engaged in unorganised sector in our country and abroad.

The studies of International Labour Organisation (I.L.O) in Ghana and Kenya initiated the proceedings of study about the unorganised sector abroad. Mention may also be made of other famous studies in Africa and Latin America such as Bunster (1983), House (1984), Rossine and Thomas (1990), Tannen (1991) etc. All these studies have explained the importance of unorganised sector in less developed countries (LDCs). They have also explained the role played by the workers engaged in this sector in developing the economy.

In India too, several studies at the conceptual level have been undertaken. In this context, the studies worth mentioning are: Bose (1974), Lubell (1974), Dipak Majumdar (1976), Breman (1976), Banerjee (1976), Joshi and Joshi (1976), Sethuraman (1975, 1976 and 1977), D'Souza (1978), Papola (1980), Desai and Krishnaraj (1982), Rajula Devi (1985) etc. The theoretical studies of Jagannathan (1987), Datta Chaudhuri (1989), Sudha Kumari (1989) and M.R. Gupta (1991) etc. have explained the policy implications and have given suggestions to make the unorganised sector in less developed countries competitive with the organised sector. Other famous studies are Sengupta, Padmini (1960), Kamal Nath (1965), Majumdar, Deepak (1973), Bhalla (1973), Bardhan (1979), Papola, T.S. (1980), Manushi (1983), Manohar (1983), Manohar and Shoba (1983), Joshi H. (1984), Arunachalam (1984), Premi M.K.(1986), Rukmani and Husain (1987), Saran and Sandhwar (1990), Sultana (1994), David (1996), Visaria (1997), Jhabvala, Renana (1988), Unni, Jeemol (1998), Gajalakshmi (1998), Papola and Sharma (1999), Malik (1999), Chadha (1999), Banerjee, Nirmala (1999), Kalpagam (1999), U. Sarkar (1999), Shaizad Suhail (1999), Srinivasan, M.V. (2000), Singh A (2000), Venkatesh, Warlu and Carta (2001) etc. Some of these studies are summarised below.

Sen Gupta, Padmini (1960), studied the position of women workers in factories, mines, agriculture, trade, professions and services. According to her, there has been a relative increase in the number of working women in agriculture, particularly when the work opportunities outside agriculture decline. She further says that women are largely employed in unskilled jobs due to their backwardness, religious and traditional conditions, illiteracy and cultural factors. Though the employment of women in certain industries has declined, but she claims that opportunities are opening up in new industries and in other fields such as tobacco, chemicals, handlooms, handicrafts, teaching, nursing, village rural works, social works, transport and communication services, telephone operating, central and state government services and other works.

Nath, Kamal, (1965), based his study primarily on a comparison of work participation rate of urban women in 38 countries. He has described that as compared to women in other developing countries of the world, the position of women in India though not unique, it still presents certain distinctive features due to traditions, backwardness and their exploitation in Indian social life. In all the ages, the reason for the low status of women belonging to lower strata is one and the same.

The changes in the society have not affected their position. The women now work in diverse fields and they have occupied important positions but in general, the three decades of development have not been very kind to them. This is particularly true in case of the women working in the unorganised sector.

Gadgill (1965): The participation of women in agricultural activities is too low because majority of older women go to the field to pick cotton, bring fuel and vegetables for the home and fodder for livestock.

Sen (1970): The study was conducted on three states. The finding of this study reveals that the unemployment of women is acute but diverse in nature.

Bhathayan (1972): Rural women work during peak season for 8-9 hours in agriculture and 4 hours in household chores as against 5 hours during ordinary days.

Majumdar, Deepak (1973) has described that organised sector provides stable and protected employment, while in the unorganised sector, workers depend on the whims of employers and they are exposed to uncertainty. He has argued that entry into the unorganised labour market is unrestricted whereas artificially raised hiring standards, norms and procedures restrict entry in the organised labour market.

Bhalla (1973) observed that the share of women as unpaid family labourer is lowest in regions where total demand for labour is very high. It is because medium and big farmers employ women labourers for harvesting and other allied operations. This trend proves that women respond to whatever will maximize their family incomes.

Bose, Ashish (1974), has pointed out that the process of urbanization has been essentially a process of migration to the cities. The cities can provide employment in the unorganised sector to rural migrants who are largely unskilled and illiterate.

Singh (1974): In India, a majority of women labourers (61 percent) are in young age group of 13-15 years engaged in farming. Out of them 90 to 96 percent working women belong to lower castes.

John Weeks (1975): The distinction between formal and unorganised sector is based on the organizational characteristics of exchange relationship and position of economic activities vis-à-vis state.

Deepak Majumdar (1975): The distinction sharply focusing on the fact that entry in to unorganised sector labour market is unrestricted whereas formal sector labour market is restricted by artificially raised standards, norms and procedures.

Kathleen Cough (1975): In some primitive societies from the very beginning women have been subordinate to men in certain key areas of status, mobility and public leadership.

Majumdar and Seth Uaman (1977) have agreed that the primary reason for rural- urban migration is economic, and the rural poor migrate to the cities in search of employment rather than for better employment opportunities. In this connection, a study of Birla Institute of Scientific Research (1980), has argued in favour of the positive contribution made by this sector. This study reveals that the unorganised sector is marked by significant turnovers both in occupations and labour mobility.

Burdhan (1979) using ordinary least squares (OLS) method for agricultural women workers in rural areas of West Bengal, analysed participation rate and labour supply functions. The results revealed that female workers participation was positively associated with lower caste families, widowed or divorced or separated women and the busy season. However, it was negatively influenced by number of dependents, number of adult males in household, family standard of living and village unemployment rate.

Papola, T.S. (1980) defined that the unorganised sector is a convenient way of designing a segment of the economy which has certain characteristics that lead to unfavourable conditions for the growth of enterprises and activities operating in this sector of the economy. He has described the following features of unorganised sector:

1. Small size of operation,
2. Unorganised structure and family ownership,
3. Non-modern technology,
4. Lack of access to government favours,
5. Unprotected labour market.

In his opinion, if the Government measures are taken to improve the working conditions in unorganised sector, this sector, may look the characteristics of its "unorganisedity."

Manohar (1983), in his study had revealed the exploitation of women in unorganised sector with reference to male dominance. He stated that women were forced to live under miserable economic and social conditions as they were subservient and dependent. The economic difficulties and poverty also forced them to work in menial and low paid jobs as the education was not required there. He had concluded that most of the women workers were employed in 'Biri' industry, cotton works, weaving and spinning works, and as domestic services etc.

Manohar and Shoba (1983) studied the problems of women working as maid servants in Warangal city (Andhra Pradesh). These women belonged to backward classes and they were working in houses of upper middle class and high economic strata families. They started working at early age. Most of them were either illiterate or at the most attained literacy up to primary level. These women workers were earning ₹ 150 per month on an average and they were mainly working as part time workers. Further, the families of these women were generally helpless, illiterate, under debt and the family income was meagre.

Joshi, H. (1984), has discussed the growing female labour force of adult women and the need for accelerated recruitment of women as compared to urban employment. He has observed that the population growth in cities is due to migration and when women join the migration stream, the demographic forces make them away from the adult male domination. He has also said that the educated women are more inclined to join the labour market. The negative factors of women's labour force are cultured resistance and lack of job opportunities.

Arunachalam (1984), expressed that women in the unorganised sector in rural areas experience various hardships in their struggle for survival. Their work roles are very seriously affected due to sex linked discriminatory injustice and heavy burden of social responsibilities. This state of affair is responsible for their male nutrition, ill health, lack of awareness about medical facilities etc. These are the causes of low economic return of women.

Bhiswanger and Rosenzweig (1984), opined that social norms affecting decisions within the family about occupational choices or migration can also lead to differential patterns of male and female earnings in unorganised markets.

Premi, M.K. (1986), described that the rapid urbanisation and the growth of population in the cities of India is due to political factors. In most cities, the sex ratio among the lifetime migrant was favourable to women but job opportunities were largely for males. Immigrants to cities from rural areas constituted 53.3 percent and from urban areas 48.8 percent. Comparatively the new cities had the highest proportion of lifetime migrant.

He has stated that young migrants from urban areas are more than those from rural areas. The proportion of rural migrants in the primary and secondary sectors is higher but urban migrants are more absorbed in tertiary sector. The author has disclosed in his study that the proportion of migrant workers in white-collar jobs is higher than non-migrants. The occupational clarification of the migrant and non-migrant workers for certain cities has indicated this result.

Devi (1986), observed in her study that in comparison to women farmers the number of agriculture women labourers was found in increasing trend. She also made it clear that they did not get their wages properly form land owners.

Rukmini and Husain (1987), after studying the nature of home based working women in garment export industry in Delhi concluded that the women working in various types of works for this industry get low wages, work for long hours in inhuman conditions and face exploitation. These women work at their homes, which are situated in slum areas with few facilities and almost no municipal amenities. These women contribute to their family income considerably. They generally work at home on piece rate basis to earn their livelihood. The cheap labour is provided by these women because they earn while sitting at home. The threat of losing the employment has forced them to accept meagre wages in the industry. These women work under tension and get no recognition for their work.

Jagan Nathan's Study (1987), seems to be a landmark in the context on unorganised sector analysis. He has developed a conceptual framework in assessing the true potential of an urban unorganised sector.

According to him, the small-scale enterprises of unorganised sector of many developing countries have contributed to increase in both private and social wealth. He has also held the opinion that although employment and wealth are generated in the urban unorganised sector, there are no institutional mechanisms available to ensure equitable diffusion. He is, thus, in favour of a practical policy that encourages diffuse urbanization, by which the flexible adaptive manufacturing enterprises of the unorganised sector can be encouraged in small rural towns and large villages. This policy involves encouraging sub-contracting in rural areas or smaller districts or sub-regional towns, so that labour can secure the benefits of economic growth without having to shift residence to overcrowded cities. This policy of diffuse urbanization, according to him would be far less expensive than the massive infrastructural investments required tackling the manifold problem of rural poverty.

Castells and Portes (1989) state that the most central

feature of unorganised sector activities is that they are unregulated by the institutions of society, in a legal and social environment in which similar activities are regulated.

Malik (1989), has stated that dalit women are forced to perform various menial tasks for upper class women. Such women are after forced to use those fields that belong to upper classes. This has made them susceptible to physical and mental harassment. He has also revealed that rape is very common for Dalit Women. In rural and urban parts of North India, women workers generally suffer from harassment though a comprehensive legislation, the Scheduled Castes and Scheduled Tribes (Prevention of) Atrocities Act, 1989 exists. This Act is in ineffective due to social, political and economic pressures. In India about two-thirds of the female population is illiterate. This is the main reason for atrocities on women even in the best urban localities.

Saran and Sandhwar (1990) studied the problems of the women workers engaged in unorganised sectors of brick kilns, quarries and mines of Bihar and West Bengal. The study revealed that the women working in these sectors are paid low wages and exploited. The migrants of them work for 14 to 16 hours and local workers 8 to 10 hours. These working women belong to Schedule castes, Schedule Tribes and backward classes. They are illiterate and indebted. The authors have also stated that the cases of rebuking, threatening, beating, cheating and sexual harassment are very common there. The women working in these sectors reported these features.

Dey B. (1993): Due to poverty, unemployment and illiteracy agriculture labourers were facing so many problems and some time the behaviour of the land owner's was not good. They were also exploited by land owners.

Turnham (1993) estimated the proportion of unorganised employment for groups of countries at different levels of development and found that the share of unorganised employment declines as the level of development rises. His definition of unorganised sector employment included wage workers in small enterprises and the self-employed excluding professionals and technicians. Recently, governments and international organizations have emphasized the dynamic features of the unorganised sector and its job creating aspect.

Portes (1994) and Assaad (1997), emphasized that it is non-compliance with the legal and administrative regulations rather than with social regulations that is important. The early development literature assumed that in the developing countries the unorganised sector would disappear over time as it did in the developed countries.

Sultania (1994) conducted a mine-level study in the major parts of Jaipur city on the women workers engaged as contract labourers. The study was based on the causes of inequality of women as contract labourers. It was find out that the construction was the main industry employing workers on contract basis. The women workers there faced socio-economic and sexual exploitation. These women were illiterate, getting low wages, working for 10-12 hours a day and experiencing male dominance. Moreover, no medical or leave facilities were availed by them. Thus, they were working under pitiable conditions.

International Labour Organisation (1995) concluded that the unorganised sector is made up of very small-scale units producing and distributing goods and services and owned and operated by largely independent, self-employed producers employing family labour or a few hired workers and apprentices. Unorganised sector enterprises are extremely diverse and are to be found in great numbers in all the main economic sectors, most of all in trade and services but also in manufacturing, construction, transport etc. They operate with very little capital or none at all, and utilise a low level of technology and skills. Employment in these enterprises is highly unstable and incomes are generally very low and irregular.

United Nations Centre, Gigiri, Kenya (1995), examined that the unorganised sector has acquired great significance over the years as a source of employment and livelihood for an increasing number of people, especially women, in both rural and urban areas of the developing world. It has particularly become a key mechanism for distributing goods and services to the urban poor.

The involvement of large number of women in the so-called 'unorganised sector' is a result of their low status in society and denial of opportunities in the organised sphere of employment. Women's low status is evidenced by their subordinate roles both at home and at the workplace. Within the organised sector, for example, women have fewer employment opportunities, lower wages and less job security than men. Moreover, women also occupy multiple roles. Many urban women, for example, work a full day either in wage-employment or in the unorganised sector and then return home to long hours of domestic labour. Women and girls who leave the rural areas in search of opportunities in urban areas tend to find employment in the least paid, least skilled jobs, which often offer little legal protection, such as domestic work (the biggest employer of women in many developing countries) or work in the unorganised sector.

According to The United Nations Fourth World Conference on Women, Beijing, China (1995), in many regions, women's participation in remunerated work in the organised and non-organised labour market has increased significantly and has changed during the past decade. While women continue to work in agriculture and fisheries, they have also become increasingly involved in micro, small and medium-sized enterprises and, in some cases, have become more dominant in the expanding unorganised sector. Due to, inter alia, difficult economic situations and a lack of bargaining power resulting from gender inequality, many women have been forced to accept low pay and poor working conditions and thus have often become preferred workers. On the other hand, women have entered the workforce increasingly by choice when they have become aware of and demanded their rights. Some have succeeded in entering and advancing in the workplace and improving their pay and working conditions.

David (1996) in his study discussed the structure and composition of urban unorganised sector. According to him the unorganised sector faces two major problems. Firstly, the large segment of work population, in this sector, is forced to live at minimum level of survival and secondly as the cheap labour is available in this sector; employers divert their activities to such organisations. The unorganised sectors are construction work, small industrial units like domestic match sticks, beedi making, food processing units and other units. These units were employing workers by low wages, low capital investments and crude technology.

The unorganised sector (non-institutionalised) also comprises workers doing casual work like the domestic servants, scavenges, sweepers, vendors, hawkers and the self employed. The women working in this sector get no security and no legal protection. They work for long hours and are exploited easily.

Joseph, E. (1997) opined that education and experience are the two of the most important factors that affect the earnings. The change in education makes more and more people receive higher education. Moreover, women's labour force participation is increased and intermittence in women job period is reduced. Female got gains in education and experience more than men did, which will help decline the gender wage gap. But the women suffered a large loss in unmeasured gender-specific factors, which reflected an increase in wage discrimination against women. Since the loss offset the woman's gain, the gender wage gap remained at its previous level.

Visaria (1997), finds that in India the incidence of discrimination is much higher in rural areas there in urban areas. He has pointed out that for all manual operations; men are paid higher wages than women. In organised sectors, there are more or less fixed salary scales but in unorganised sector women workers suffer in earnings. In employment discrimination against women has continued as they get lower wages. In this matter the law of equal pay for equal work has not been enforced. Women are employed as daily rated workers and are not promoted to the supervisory category. Similarly, a large number of women are employed in the small-scale sector or in home based industries but not males. The women are, thus, exploited both on wages and conditions of work.

He has also stated that many divorced, widowed and separated women are exploited both socially and economically. They face insecurity and intolerable hardships. As most policies are male dominated, the adequate provisions for women are lacking, though they play a dual role as worker and as home maker.

Jhabvala Renana (1998), emphasized the need for social security for women workers in unorganised sector. In this study, the mechanism for security provisions, insurance and security funds for women workers in unorganized sector was explored. It was also pointed out that the women of unorganised sector could be helped by decentralising, participatory social security and implementation of programmes. For women in unorganised sector, the employment based programmes should have social and financial security.

Unni Jeemol (1998), reviewed the concept of unorganised sector and methodologies for estimation of labour force and contribution to Gross Domestic Product. It has been stated that unorganised sector and other hidden economic activities have become prominent in the context of structural adjustment and globalisation. Work of unorganised sector workers especially of women should be recognised since their employment in unorganised sector is significant and maximum.

Gajalakshmi (1998) in her study dealt with women workers employed in unorganised sector of shoe factories in

Tamil Nadu. The study is empirical in nature. The women working in these factories belong to backward classes and scheduled castes. These women are paid low wages and thus, they live in poverty. Their educational level is low and they work for long hours. The main aim of their occupation in this job is to supplement their low family income.

Gurung (1999), focused that in general, rural women's work patterns are marked by change and continuity as well as flexibility and rigidity. Change and flexibility are characterized by women taking on new roles in farm production, off-farm production and community production to ensure the family's access to food and household resources. Continuity and rigidity relate to social norms that define gender roles and dictate that rural women and girls should assume home production responsibilities in rural households. The intra-household decisions on allocation of labour often are biased and relegate domestic tasks to women and girls. In the region, tradition driven socialization defines the tasks and taboos in the economic and social spheres among rural women. Increasingly, faced with economic pressures, gender roles may become flexible to enable women to engage in work traditionally regarded as belonging in the male domain. However, the rigid gender role definitions dictate that men should not perform household tasks. A pattern of gender roles marked by diversity in flexibility and change as well as convergence in rigidity and continuity is described with illustrations from various countries.

Papola and Sharma (1999), focused that in the unorganised sector, there is a marginal increase of participation of women workers. In this sector, gender discrimination for worker is more prevalent. However, government organisations, non-government organisations and women activists, who are strengthening women capabilities and increasing work opportunities, will reduce imbalances and bring gender equity in employment.

Ranis and Stewart (1999) examined the unorganised sector

in relation to the rest of the economy and divided it into two parts, a modernizing dynamic component and a traditional stagnant one.

Banerjee, Nirmala (1999), stated that women in many parts of India have no knowledge, skill or information about the charges that are taking place. The problems of illiteracy, caste-based exploitation and poverty are further compounded in case of women due to bindings put on them by their own families under sanctions from the entire society.

She has also stated that women's fight for emancipation and empowerment cannot start till they are regarded more than a flexible resource at the disposal of the household. Their options outside marriage have been ruined by their socialisation. The options given to them merely increase their workload. They do nothing for their empowerment.

Kalpagam (1999), revealed that women, both rural and urban are engaged predominantly in domestic duties. They are also engaged in other works that are beneficial for the household. The desire of these women to access cash income has compelled them to take up domestic duties. He has also stated that the need is to make access to cash income possible for women.

Sarkar (1999), stated that the low level of literacy and social status keeps the women workers in inferior status. The inferior status of women at work has further enforced their inferior status in the society. At work they are rarely promoted to the sub-staff. Their involvement in the trade union movement has been limited due to low level literacy.

Shaizad Suhail (1999), concluded that 95 percent of working women surveyed had some form of sexual harassment at their work place. It has also been stated in the study that 55 percent of them simply ignored such harassment and only 10 percent actually filed complaints with police.

Chadha (1999), undermined the importance of acquiring education and skills to overcome the discrimination that the rural women in agriculture face on this labour market.

According to him for a shift from agriculture to non-agriculture jobs, women require proper education. He has also noted that the difference in male-female wages is widest at the level of illiterate workers. The state of wage differential can be totally obliterated at higher educational levels.

Srinivasan, M.V. (2000), discussed the conceptual issued of the unorganised sector and the trend of women's employment. He has concluded that employment for the unorganised women workers moves to such sectors where they have no say at all and there is no legal protection for them. In India, the surplus labour in agricultural sector could not pick up non-farm employment, which was hailed as the panacea for them. The most affected are women.

Singh, A. (2000), reported in his study that the economic hardships to lower, middle and working class women and the growing economic crisis in India have initiated the working women to organise themselves to save them from worsening economic situation.

Agrawal, Meenu (2000), said that there are two main factors for determining the status of women in any society, particularly in traditional societies like India. The status of women particularly in unorganized sector is much more disadvantageous in term of share in equality of life indicators. She revealed that the problems of poverty can't be tackled without providing opportunities to productive employment to women. It may be stated that productive employment to women would provide necessary economic base & improve their social status.

Gaur K.D. and Rachita Rana (2000), emphasised that majority of women work in unorganised sector for low wages because of low level of skills, very high level of exploitation, illiteracy, ignorance and surplus labour. This hampers the bargaining power for increase in wages, remuneration not compatible to hours of work put in and any opportunity for further development. These factors are the root causes for prevalence of child labour. Such uncared children are subjected to all sorts of violence viz. social, mental and physical. The mental block that literacy does not guarantee job, it is an unnecessary investment with no returns and along with hassles of admission at schools, discourage children enrolments at schools. Thus, it can be stated that 'illiteracy breeds illiteracy'.

Venkatesh Warlu and Carta (2001), highlighted the relevance and accountability of women workers. They have concluded in their study that women workers are indispensable for the stability of agricultural sector.

Agrawal Meenu (2003), said in her study that women perform agricultural operations with the use of traditional tools and implements. In present time women are engaged in livestock, forestry, fishing, plantation, orchard and allied activities. Now the participation of rural women in agriculture is increasing in spite of scientific and technological developments in agriculture.

The average time spent by a farm-woman varies from village to village according to social customs. But the women hands are invisible even to this day, so it seems looking at the agricultural extension activities, which are mainly a male-oriented pursuit.

Agrawal R. C. (2003), reported in his study that the success of economic development depends, to a great extent, upon the active involvement of both men and women. It requires shunning off the age-old traditions and orthodox thinking, which reduces women only as household maid-servants or a decorative piece within or outside our houses. If the rural women continue to be left out of the main stream of economic development and they are deprived of opportunities to realize their full potential, serious inefficiencies in the use of resources will persist.

Singh, Gopal and Singh, Asmita (2003), highlighted that unorganised sector of the economy provides big employment opportunities to women workers in India, but unfortunately even after five decades of planned development the status and working condition of rural women in this sector is pitiable. The rural women are usually illiterate, unskilled and totally exploited. Being poor and desperate for job they agree on any terms and conditions offered to them regarding work conditions, risks involved and wages. Usually, such women are the sole bread earners for their families. All this clearly points out the low status of rural women in India.

Baruah Bipasha (2004), examined that it is now widely understood that the needs of women workers in the unorganised sector are not met by the conservative practices of labour organizations and trade unions. While the contribution of women to the economies of developing countries is crucial, women rarely find employment in the regulated unionized sectors of these countries, and are found instead in overwhelming numbers in the sector that is variously termed 'unorganized', 'unprotected', or 'unregistered'.' This article addresses the situation of women in the unorganised economy in South Asia. The author explores the major challenges and opportunities facing women in their efforts to organize and mobilize for change. She also provides a critical analysis of the different types of interventions adopted by the state and civil society organizations in South Asia to empower women in the unorganised sector. The author concludes with an attempt to identify the mix of interventions and strategies most needed for different social, political and economic circumstances.

Selçuk Fatma Ülkü (2005), stated that the number of unorganized women and child workers has increased rapidly. Working hours and labour laws have become more "flexible." Order-based production has destroyed job security. Full-time, regular employment has been gradually replaced by part-time, temporary, and precarious work. Thus, the unorganised sector (which encompasses child labour, migrant workers, temporary workers, contract workers, domestic workers, home workers, and workers in small production units and subcontractor firms) has become more and more prevalent around the world.

Although it has not been long since the trade unions

started organizing in the unorganised sector, there are countries where this has been successful. India is one of these countries, and it has a wealth of experience in organizing the unorganized. The Chhattisgarh Mine Workers Union (CMWU) of India is also an example of organizing in the unorganised sector. Indeed, their organizational experiences in the unorganised sector offer important clues and lessons for the future. It is clear that unless unions develop effective forms of struggle, they will sooner or later vanish from the scene of history. Yet, there is hope and it is growing stronger. If unions organize the unemployed and the unorganised sector workers, they can present a serious challenge to the anti-union current and start healing the wounds of the labour movement.

Ramachandran S. (2006), pointed out that it is now accepted that the participation of women themselves in development activities is the most effective tool for the promotion of the access of women to the benefits of development. In the economic sphere, women have fewer opportunities than men, they earn about half of men's income, and they have particularly no ownership of resources. The problem is mainly the limited mobility of women, which does not allow them access to improved opportunities in skill development or economic betterment. It is also revealed that in most sectors of the economy, women tend to be employed in the low paid, most menial tasks, using the least technology. For example, in agriculture women engage in labour intensive tasks such as transplantation and weeding.

Rengarajan, S. (2006) has concluded that women have key role to play in unorganised sectors throughout the world. Rural women play two major roles in rural areas- household responsibilities for child rearing, food preparation and other chores, and the other role they are paid or unpaid workers in agriculture or off the farm. At present, in rural India about 33 percent of cultivators and about 47 percent of agricultural labourers are women.

Singh, B.N. (2006), concluded in his study that the present

status of women in agriculture—has the utmost need to revamp the entire approach towards women farmers to cater to their existing needs. There is no alternative way but to develop the human resource. It is also liable to develop the Indian agriculture by way of making women partners in development and brining them in the mainstream of development not only as beneficiaries but also as contributors.

Arvind (2007) proposed that while India strives to create more jobs with social security and health-care benefits in the organised sector; the proportion of people employed in the unorganised sector has swelled. In 2004-05, the latest government numbers show, the proportion of people employed in the unorganised sector had risen by 8.4 percent from 1999-2000. This data comes from the latest survey on unorganised sector employment conditions, conducted in 2004-05 by the National Sample Survey Organization (NSSO). The percentage of unorganised sector workers has grown 10 percent in rural areas and 6.1 percent in urban areas, or from 691 of every 1,000 persons in 1999-2000 to 749 for every 1,000 in 2004-05, most have no access to any form of social security. "There is need for steps to accelerate growth in the organized sector, or factories, and at the same time, develop some social security measures for unorganised sector workers and the self-employed," said minister of state for commerce, Jairam Ramesh.

D.P. Singh (2007) reveals that the life of the women workers in brick kilns industry is very tough. These women have to perform a dual role relating to production and reproduction. While bearing and rearing children remain their primary responsibility, they are invariably involved in the remunerative activities also. These women are unprotected and suffer from economic exploitation. Their ignorance, illiteracy and poverty have added to their woes all the more. A great majority of them have not been benefited by the protective legislation in the critical areas of wages, maternity benefits, childcare and social security. It attempts to identify and understand the problems of these workers besides looking into effectiveness of various welfare legislations, besides exploring the possibilities and prospects for ameliorating their living standards.

Balbir Soni (2007), explained that women constitute a large majority of the labour force in the rural areas of the least developed countries, particular attention has to be paid to women's development in terms of adequate mother and child health care, introduction of local technologies to make women's work less burdensome, and above all to provide the basic necessities such as clean drinking water and fuel for home use in order to reduce dramatically the time that is spent at present on these tasks.

The empowerment of women workers, particularly in the unorganised sector, has been discussed at length in the present publication. It profiles such important issues such as: current trends of employed women in the international context; tribal women and their participation in development, marginalised women workers and government initiatives in economic empowerment among others.

Santosh Nandal (2007), concluded that a vast majority of India's labour force is in unorganized sector. In the absence of economic opportunities in their own states, many workers migrate across the other states of India to seek employment. Construction industry depends almost entirely on migrant workers, majority of which are women. The main object of this paper is to shed light on the socio-economic problems being faced by a section of the women workers in construction industry. These women workers have a very tough life. In spite of being actively involved in economic activities for survival, bearing and rearing of children remain their prime responsibility, and thus, they end up with playing roles in both production and reproduction.

Singh, J.L. and Pandey, R.K, (2007), explained that women entered the market for wage labour after the industrial revolution, creating employment opportunities for women.

Their significance was considered marginal and constituted the reserved labour force. They entered the labour market only when the economic necessities forced them to supplement the meagre family earnings. The labouring women generally work in the unorganised sector.

Rajalakshmi, T.K. (2007), explained that the Bill that the government finally introduced to safeguard the interests of workers in the unorganised sector is a disappointment.

Archana, Sinha, (2008), pointed out that women constitute the largest segment of India's unorganised sector in the country. Many workers in the unorganised sector lack access to even information about basic rights like minimum wages. Their wages and earnings are generally at mere survival level. They do not get protection of labour laws due to ignorance and weak enforcement. The unorganised workers are generally denied social security, welfare and health covers. They are engaged in unorganised economic activities which encompasses small scale industries, cottage industries, micro units of production, construction, in large manufacturing units, textile and garment, horticulture, agriculture, rural occupations, forest based employment's, fisheries, sweeping-cleaning, loading-unloading, mining, forestry, service sector, entertainment, etc.

The globalisation influenced policies of the government have led to increased contractual? In unorganised sector closure of small-scale industries and so the size of unorganised sector workers is growing at a faster rate. A rough estimate would suggest 94 percent of approximately 405 million are in unorganised or informal sector. Women who work on work sites like construction work or brick kilns face problems of child care, have no toilet or drinking water facilities and are vulnerable to sexual exploitation. Some, like domestic workers, are not even recognised as workers in the law.

Deprivations and vulnerability are integral to the lives of many millions of unorganised workers. Social security benefits are essentially a part of universal human rights. In India which is the largest democracy in the world, social protection remains the biggest challenge. The unorganised sector in India is deprived of these benefits. India is a nation with one-sixth of the world human population. The social security measures planned and implemented in India in the post-Independence era have been limited to organised sectors whereas the majority of the work force earns wages through unorganised sectors. The Government of India has been dealing with a population that has been ever growing. The planners with the limited resources have barely been able to cope with the ever increasing demands. The real challenge is to ensure that the labour laws and social security schemes that exist for workers in the organised sector are extended and implemented to the workers in the unorganised sector. Government institutions and NGOs need to build up a system in order to build in community-based network.

Arani Sinha (2008), pointed out that in India, almost 92 percent of the work force is in the unorganized sector, one-third of which are women and their dependents. Though the Indian Constitution guarantees equality of opportunity related to work, equal rights for livelihood, equal pay for equal work etc, the condition of women in the unorganized sector is deplorable. Majority of women in the unorganized sector work for low and highly unequal wages compared to their male counterparts. The unorganized sector as it is, is characterized by no clear cut relationship between the employer and the employee as most of the employees are contractual, casual, migrants, home based etc. Because of this character of employees the safeguard of the rights of employees, social security protection, labour laws are not applicable in the unorganized sector. Thus, the workers in the unorganized sector in general are outside the purview of Protective Labour Laws and Trade Union Organizations. In this context the condition of women who are exploited even in organized sector, is worse in the unorganized sectors.

Muthusamy Eswari (2009) has concluded that it is an open

truth that working women have to face problems just by virtue of their being women. Working women here are referred to those who are in paid employment. Social attitude to the role of women lags much behind the law. This attitude which considers women fit for certain jobs and not others colours those who recruit employees.

Devika P. (2010), revealed that unorganised sector is referred to as the unorganized sector. This sector broadly corresponds to the household sector including private unincorporated enterprises. The unorganized sector also includes some formal activities on which there is no regular system of data availability. However, contribution of these formal activities in the unorganized sector is quite small. The term unorganised sector was coined by the British economist Keith Hart in 1971, the fact remains that it has emerged as a dynamic and vibrant sector, representing a growing proportion of economic activity, particularly in the developing countries.

Pandya, Rameshwari and Patel, Sarika (2010), opined, according to the final report of the National Commission for Enterprises in the unorganised Sector (NCEUS) released in April 2009, workers in the unorganized sector constitute more than 93 percent of the total workforce of India. Unorganized sector workers are those who do not have any job security, income security or social security and are therefore extremely vulnerable to exogenous shocks. The problems of women workers in general and in the unorganised sector in particular deserve special emphasis and focus in view of their marginalised position within the class of workers. Even when women are not employed in the sense of contributing to the national output, a considerable share of their time is consumed by socially productive and reproductive labour. This is what is called the double burden of work that distinguishes women from men. A number of national and international studies have documented the sex-typing of jobs and occupations by women. Sexual division of labour has implications for the wages earned, permanency in the job and the possibilities for upward mobility in the industry. The overall picture that emerges is one of greater disadvantage for women workers in general and those belonging to rural as well as Scheduled Caste /Scheduled Tribes in particular.

Terrell McSweeny (2010), quoted, that yesterday I picked up my Wall Street Journal and read an opinion piece "Washington's Equal Pay Obsession" arguing that the Paycheck Fairness Act is unnecessary because, in a nutshell, women don't face rampant pay discrimination. Instead, the author asserted, the wage gap exists because women are mothers. So let's break this down. First, there is ample evidence that women–regardless of their parental status— do face pay discrimination. Yes, part of the wage gap was a result of occupational choices and other factors.

Newstrack India, Lucknow, (2010), commented, when we talk of India's mammoth work force, be it in rural or urban scenarios, what comes to mind is the 'unorganised' sector? They form the multitudes that do not 'belong' to a sector governed by a slew of measures in accordance with labour laws or employment terms defined by policy measures. These are the multitudes, which fall outside the ambit of Central Government legislation pertaining to wages and salaries. They are covered by the laws of the state governments. In an urban scenario the two sectors stand out distinctly.

Most of the studies on women workers in unorganised sector are at macro level and there are such studies conducted at micro level also. In some studies there is a segregation of rural and urban sectors. The studies have highlighted the pitiable condition of these women and have suggested measures for improvement in their conditions. But no study has been conducted on the role and problems of working women in unorganised sector in small cities and towns.

3

Characteristics of Unorganized Sector/Labour

3.1 Conceptual Framework

The term 'unorganised labour' has been defined as those workers who have not been able to organize themselves to pursue their common interests due to certain constraints like casual nature of employment, ignorance and illiteracy, small and scattered size of establishments, etc.

The workers in unorganised sector fall in various categories but a large number of them are home-based workers who are engaged in occupations like beedi rolling, agarbatti making, papad making, tailoring, and zari embroidery etc.

As per the survey carried out by the National Sample Survey Organisation in the year 2004-2005, the total employment, in both organised and unorganised sectors in the country was of the order of 45.9 crore, i.e., around 2.6 crore in the organised sector and the balance 43.3 crore in the unorganised sector.

In order to take care of the social security and welfare of unorganised workers, two-pronged strategy, i.e., legislative measures, and, implementation of welfare schemes and programmes have been followed so far.

The legislative measures include the Minimum Wages Act, 1948, the Workmen's Compensation Act, 1923, the Maternity Benefit Act, 1961, the Bonded Labour System (Abolition) Act, 1976, the Contract Labour (Regulation and Abolition) Act, 1970, the Inter-State Migrant Workmen (Regulation of Employment and Conditions of Service) Act, 1979, the Building and Other Construction Workers (Regulation of Employment and Conditions of Service) Act, 1996, etc.

The Government has set up welfare funds for providing welfare measures to the *beedi*, non-coal mine and mine workers. The funds are used to provide financial assistance to these workers for education of their children, recreation, medical and health facilities, construction of houses, etc.

The Building and Other Construction Workers (Regulation of Employment and Conditions of Service) Act, 1996 also has provision for setting up of welfare board/fund by every State Government to provide welfare/social security measures to the construction workers. Some States like Kerala have constituted welfare funds for specific categories of workers in the unorganised sector.

The Government enacted the Unorganised Workers' Social Security Act, 2008. The Act provides for constitution of National Social Security Board at the Central level and State Social Security Boards at the State level which shall recommend formulation of social security schemes for unorganised workers.

The National Board shall recommend social security schemes viz., life and disability cover, health and maternity benefits; old age protection, and any other benefit as may be determined by the Central Government.

The State-level Boards shall recommend welfare schemes viz. provident fund, employment injury benefit, housing, educational schemes for children, skill up gradation of workers, funeral assistance; and old age homes of bonded labourers once in 3 years in a district and ₹ 5.00 lakh per annum for conducting evaluatory studies. So far 2,68,136 identified bonded labourers have been rehabilitated with the Central assistance of ₹ 6,983 lakh.

According to National Commission on Labour (1966-69) "Unorganised labour are those who, on account of certain constraints such as illiteracy and ignorance of workers, casual nature of employment, small size and scattered establishments and position of power enjoyed by the employers, have not been able to organise themselves, in pursuit of common objectives." [1] As a matter of fact, it is very difficult to give a precise definition of the unorganised sector because of wide diversity in this sector and the decentralisation of its works. Any attempt to define unorganised sector as a separate category and distinguish it from organised sector cannot be fruitful because it is very difficult to identify common characteristics of a particular set of workers in the labour market.

Women are usually employed in different sectors than men. Most of women's non agricultural employment is in the service sector. But in developing countries female employment in manufacturing has been increasing and is catching up with female employment in services (ILO/INSTRAW, 1985). Women in manufacturing tend to be concentrated in only a few sub sectors: more than two-thirds of the global labour force in garment production is female and this sub-sector absorbs almost one-fifth of the female labour force in manufacturing (UNIDO, 1993). Men's employment is more evenly distributed across other sectors such as mining manufacturing, construction and transport.

Over their lifetime, women change their employment status more often than do men. They are also more likely to be self-employed or employed in occupations with flexible house such as sub-contracted home work. Regardless of the sector in which they are employed, women tend to work in a narrow range of occupations.

Only a few women are in high-paying jobs or in positions with significant responsibility. Nearly two-thirds of the women in manufacturing are labourers, machine operators and production workers; only 5 percent are professional and technical workers and only 2 percent are administrators and managers (UNIDO, 1993). However, there are regional differences: women occupy nearly 60 percent of clerical, sales and service jobs in Latin America and the Caribbean but fewer than 20 percent of similar positions in South Asia, North Africa and the Middle East.

Significant changes in the global economy have affected patterns of employment and working conditions for men and women worldwide. "Globalization" is associated with the deregulation of product and labour markets, with regionalization and with the liberalization of international trade. In term these processes are associated with increased female participation in the labour force and with the "casualization" of employment, as seen in the growth of part-time work in industrial economies. However, the net effect of globalization on women workers is not yet clear. Growth in the international trade and service sector (for example, banking and telecommunications) seems to have offered women in developing countries greater employment opportunities. In addition, the participation rate of women in manufacturing jobs has increased faster than that of men. Women's average participation in the manufacturing labour force is now around 30 percent for both developing and industrial countries.

As regards women workers in the unorganised sector, it can be expressed that all those women, who sell their labour in cash or kind and engage themselves into some activity or work to earn their livelihood, are women workers in the unorganised sector. These women remain unorganised and work for long hours on meagre wages with no jobs security. They are not provided suitable conditions at workplace. They face ill behaviour of the employers and in some cases, even the sexual harassment and exploitation at their hands.

Although, there are no clear and precise definitions of the unorganised sector, it often refers to activities typically at a low level of organisation and technology with primary objective of generating employment and incomes. The activities are usually conducted without proper recognition from authorities and escape the attention of the administrative machinery responsible for enforcing laws and regulations. [2]

Undoubtedly, there are a number of problems in properly defining the unorganised sector. Jan Breman, in this context, has remarked, " the lack of proper definition is very often, although not very satisfactorily compensated by a somewhat arbitrary listing of those activities which meet the eye of anyone who strolls through the street of a city in Third world: street vendors, newspaper sellers, shoeshine boys, stall keepers, prostitutes, porters, beggars, hawkers rickshaw pullers etc." [3]

Thus, the unorganised sector includes those activities of small tradesmen and unskilled workers which bring them small and irregular income. Further, it consists of small scale units engaged in the production and distribution of goods and services with the primary objective of generating employment and income.

The concept of unorganised sector is not a new concept as the term informal is used alternatively. Similarly, the terms formal and organised are used interchangeably. The term 'unorganised sector' was first used by Keith Hart in 1971 in the study of the Ghana. The term meant that part of urban labour that falls outside the organised market.[4] Keith came across a large number of self employed sectors during his field work among the workers of Ghana, which provided means of livelihood to the urban labour force. These workers were new entrants who were not provided employment in the organized sector. The traditional attitude about this sector was to treat it as highly unproductive and constituting surplus labour force. Hart put this sector into unorganised sector.

He has used the terms 'unorganised sector', 'unremunerated sector', 'self-employed individuals', unorganised income generating activities and urban proletariat as more or less alternatively.

In order to understand the meaning, characteristics and scope of unorganised sector it is necessary to understand the concept of organised sector or formal sector of an economy. This sector is generally known as a sector employing workers permanently, providing regulated conditions of work, registering employees under the Factories Act, contracting wages of employment with the employers and using advanced or modern technology for production. The employer in this sector may either be a private organisation or individual or the Government. The workforce is generally skilled. The production units permit constitution of labour unions and government protection of employment. All these factors ensure that the employment of labour is secured.

Thus, the organised sector is a protected sector. It is, thus, clear that the economic activities which do not meet the aforesaid requirements are grouped under unorganised sector. In simple words, it may be said that the unorganized sector is that sector which is not organised in its character.

The working conditions in unorganised sector employment are rarely covered by the legal status and therefore, this sector is ignored by official censuses. Several empirical studies, concluded, in developing countries have focused the disadvantages of the unorganised sector primarily due to lack of access to the sources such as capital, finance, skills, modern technology etc. Thus, a segment of the economy having certain characteristics that lead to conditions not favourable for the growth of enterprises and activities operating in this segment may be conveniently designated as 'unorganised sector'. The term unorganised sector has no specific meaning in itself, it is used "for lack of a better alternatives." [4]

Kenneth King has defined unorganised sector as follows: "Their unorganisedity derives from their being unrecognised in government employment statistics and operating in the main act of the make shift shelters on urban waste lands road sides and forest fringes." [5]

"Souza and Tokman stated that this sector "comprises of all those engaged in domestic services, casual labour, the self-employed and employees of white collar, blue collar and family workers in enterprises with a total start of not more than four persons." [6]

Luball has defined that " the unorganised sector constitute the residual labour market of last resort, into which persons enter as self employed, low income producers of marginal goods and services for lack of any other means of earning as livelihood." [7]

The definitions of unorganised sector make it clear that it is an exclusive term. Normally, this sector includes petty traders, small manufacturing units, construction work, trade, transport and communication, service sectors engaged in the production of goods and services which operate on a very small scale and have no organised organisation. [8] The elements in the definitions of unorganised sector show broad spectrum of heterogeneous activities of urban and rural households. The heterogeneity of unorganised sector has initiated to search a common criterion for the identification of unorganised sector enterprises.

From the above discussion about the unorganised sector, it is clear that this sector is so vast that it cannot be confined to conceptual definition. Therefore, descriptive means can better identify the position of this sector.

As said earlier, the unorganised sector is very diverse. Many efforts have been made to identify the characteristics of employments or undertakings in the sector. But none of the characteristics can be termed as crucial in defining the sector. There are several well accepted characteristics of this sector. Therefore, to identify this sector clearly, it is necessary to discuss its characteristics in detail. The broad characteristics of unorganised sector are as follows:

Smallness is a very important characteristic of unorganised sector. This sector generally consists of small establishments. The term 'smallness', may, however, have different interpretations in different situation. The size of employment is an important factor for demarcation of this sector from other sectors. It has been expressed that self employed workers and single worker establishments generally form the unorganized sector. The unorganised sector has limited access to resources and the nature of its product is freely competitive. Due to these characteristics of this sector, its activities are covered under the small scale, operations. Thus, small scale operations form the core of the unorganised sector.

This sector uses local inputs due to small scale operations. It is, therefore, clear that 'small size of operations' is the necessary condition to include an enterprise in the unorganised sector.

3.2 Low Rate of Participation

Unpaid work and family responsibilities as well as lack of investment in women's education are strongly associated with women's relatively low rates of participation and their limited earnings in organised sector labour. Women's participation rates usually dip in the child-bearing years, and earnings tend to decline following an interruption in employment. Younger on average, work more hours than older women, and married women with young children tend to work less than childless women and mothers of grown children. The correlation of marriage and childbearing with labour market outcomes can be seen even in industrial countries, where wage differences between married women and men are larger than those between single women and men. Similarly, in some developing countries relative earnings decline with age. Children are not the only reason for interruptions in women's labour force participation; caring for ill or aged family members is often a woman's responsibility.

3.3 Low Scale of Organisation and Family Ownerships

The unorganised sector enterprises do not have an organised structured organisation. The functional division of labour is limited there and the specialisation is also ignored. The proprietors perform most of the management and supervisory functions and sometimes they also perform some of the production functions.

In unorganised sector, the family labour is also extensively used. However, this may not be true and appropriate always.

Papola has remarked that "in unorganised sector all the characteristics may not exist together. It is possible and sometimes necessary to run small size enterprises without functional diversion of labour and management hierarchy. Moreover, the enterprises with wider ownership and using hired labour may reveal these characteristics though the size of their operations is not large enough. It is also worth mentioning that in India some of the largest organisations are owned by individual families but they cannot be run on the basis of unorganised and unstructured organisation. It has been rightly said that structure of organization is mainly a function of size and is not necessarily related to the pattern of ownerships." [9]

3.4 Low Order Technology

In unorganized sector, low order technology, which prevails universally in this sector, is used. It is a predominantly labour intensive technology. This technology uses low techniques of production. Modern technology, which is used by organised sector, is capital intensive highly, productive and mechanized. It has also been stated by some authors on the subject that the concept of foreign ownership and imported technology is also recognised in case of private organised sector which produces for sophisticated markets.

Year 2011 Women's Day theme was "Equal access to education, training and science and technology: Pathway to decent work for women". The theme also marked the occasion when the three Rome-based agencies are organizing a joint event to present the publication titled State of Food and Agriculture 2010-11: Women in agriculture–closing the gender gap for development.

The characteristics of unorganised sector, on the other hand, are small-scale operation, labour intensive technology, low levels of income and indigenous ownership. [10] The question of indigenous technology is rather incidental to this issue. This technology is used in unorganized sector due to the disadvantageous position of this sector. As a matter of fact, the distinction between the unorganised and organised sectors on the basis of the use of indigenous technology and foreign technology is not worthwhile. There are some large textile industries in India which do not use foreign technology, yet they cannot be included in the unorganised sector because they have all other characteristics of organised Sector." [11]

3.5 Lack of Support from Government

Unorganised sector enterprises are not supposed to have access to public facilities and state patronage. The advantages of organised capital market, bank finance, imported raw materials, foreign technology, protection from competition from organised sector units etc. are not expected to be available to the unorganised sector. In fact, these facilities are not denied to the unorganised sector enterprises but due to their meagre material resources, they are unable to avail them. [12]

It has been seen that even when the government tried to make some of these advantages available to the unorganised sector units, by giving them a preferential treatment, the benefits have not gone to them because of their inability to cope with the difficult official procedures.

Some of the inputs services like bank finance, water, electricity, space etc. are not supported on a government license. Even these facilities are not adequately availed to the unorganised sector enterprises. In reality, it is the result of uneven distribution of the private resources which have resulted into ill distribution of the benefits of public resources. Thus, the unorganised sector units which are mostly established at backward or remote places do not generally have access to benefits of public resources.

3.6 Unregulated and Highly Competitive Labour Market

The labour market in the unorganised sector is unregulated and highly competitive as in it there is absolute freedom of entry. In the unorganised sector, the supply of labour consists mainly of new entrants or immigrants in the labour market.

These new entrants or immigrants aspire for jobs in the organised sector but the opportunities are limited and entry is restricted there. Thus, they start doing something or the other in the unorganised sector. They either by starting small business employ themselves or absorb themselves in part time jobs or as apprentices or as full time workers in small units. Thus, the unorganised sector has come into existence owing to non-availability of the work in the organised sector. The unorganised sector, therefore, suffers from the problem of excess supply of labour which tends to lead to a situation of wide prevalence of unemployment, low wages, self or casual employment. There are no work and wage regulations in this sector. The workers in this sector work for long hours on meagre wages. This sector also suffers from the vicissitudes of market fluctuations and also from whims of the employers.

In contrast to the unorganised sector, the labour market in the organised sector is regulated and has restricted entry on the basis of hiring programmes and well defined norms. Thus, in the organised sector there is no excess supply of labour. The level of wages and conditions of work are regulated and jobs are secured there.

3.7 Unprotected Product Market

The unorganised sector operates in highly competitive and unprotected markets. The goods and services produced by the sector are often sold at unfavourable conditions because it faces iniquitous competition from the organised industries. [13] As the unorganised sector establishments are very large in number, they operate in a highly competitive market. However, it is always true that unorganised sector units operate in a competitive market and all the organised sector establishments operate in a protected market. For example, the unorganised sector units which produce artistic handicraft goods, in our country operate mostly in a non-competitive market, whereas organised sector units producing textiles clothing, washing soaps, tooth pastes and brushes, vegetable oils and a number of other items of mass consumption, operate in a highly competitive markets.

It is also not always true that unorganised sector produces goods and services of general use and the organised sector mostly caters to the demand of people of high income groups and foreign markets. Services offered by the domestic servants in the urban areas, which are included in the unorganised sector activity, cater to the needs of high sections of society. Similarly, artistic handicrafts produced by the unorganised sector establishments, also support the aforesaid example.

The organised sector, on the other hand, produces many items of general use which are also produced by the unorganised sector. However, the items produced by the organised sector have the advantages of better marketing net works and the brand name etc. Moreover, the organised sector establishments realise more revenue per unit of their products then the unorganised units. As a matter of fact, unorganised sector units suffer in this respect due to their limited holding capacity and marketing arrangements.

After discussing various definitions and characteristics of unorganised sector, it may be stated that the unorganised and organised sectors are distinguished on the basis of size, organisation, technology, relations with the government and labour and product market conditions. As a matter of fact, the nature of the organised sector is capitalistic; which uses capital intensive technology for production whereas the unorganised sector generally uses labour intensive traditional technology for production. The organised sector has sufficient access to the government machinery, the unorganised sector, however, is not provided adequate protection by the government. It is also very important to point out here that workers in the organised sector have unions which are led by influential persons and politicians of various political parties whereas the unorganised sector workers almost have no unions and thus, they are exploited by their employers. Unorganised sector also suffers in the matter of institutional credit for finance as it has a very limited capacity to cope with the requirements of such institutions.

In brief the characteristics of unorganised sector are:

1. Operation of labour relations on a casual basis, or on the basis of kinship or personal relations.
2. Production expenditure indistinguishable from household expenditures and use of capital goods.
3. Easy entry and exit.
4. Free mobility within the sector.
5. Use of indigenous resources and technology.
6. Unregulated or unprotected nature.
7. Absence of fixed working hours.
8. Lack of security of employment and other social security benefits.
9. Use of labour intensive technology.
10. Lack of support from government.
11. Workers living in slums and squatter areas.
12. Lack of housing and access to urban services.
13. Low earning sector.
14. Women constitute an important section of the workers in this sector.
15. Family labour is engaged in some occupations such as home-based ones.
16. Economic activities, which engage child labour, fall within this sector.
17. Migrant labour is involved in some sub-sectors.
18. Piece-rate payment, home-based work and contractual work are increasing trends in this sector.
19. Direct recruitment is on the decline. Some employees are engaged through contractors. An increasing trend to recruit workers through contractors is visible in areas of home-based work. There is a sort of convergence of home-based work and engagement in work through contractors
20. Some kinds of employment are seasonal, some others are intermittent. As such, underemployment is a serious problem.

21. Most jobs are, for the greater part, on a casual basis.
22. Both employed and self-employed workers can be found in a number of occupations.
23. Workers are not often organised into trade unions. The self-employed are seldom organised into associations. There is not much recourse to collective bargaining.
24. There are many co-operatives of self-employed workers.
25. Very often, others supply raw materials, Production by self employed workers, therefore, becomes dependent on, or linked with enterprises or individuals active in other sectors.
26. Debt bondage is very common among the employed as well as the self-employed workers in the unorganised sector.
27. The self-employed have less access to capital. Whatever capital they manage, is mostly from non-banking and unusual sources, especially from the trader-contractor.
28. Health hazards exist in a majority of occupations.

3.8 Linkages between Organised and Unorganised Sectors

Both the organised and unorganised sectors have direct inter-linkages or inter-relationships in terms of resource inputs, technology and market approaches.

Several studies on the subject have identified the nature of relationships between the two sectors. Bose, in his study of the unorganised sector in the Calcutta Metropolitan Economy, for the International Labour Organisation, has explained the linkage between the organised and unorganised sectors in the following words:

"The casual hypothesis that this study has thrown up is that the organised and unorganised sectors operate in basically two different markets that it is the difference that mainly differentiates the unorganised sector from the organised and these two sectors are dependent upon one another in much the same way that a colonial economy and a metropolitan economy are dependent upon each other. This means that the under employment and backwardness of the unorganised sector are necessary conditions for the development and advancement of the organised formal sector dominated by a few oligopolistic owners." [14]

Bose thus places great stress saying that the development of the organised sector depends upon the backwardness and unemployment of the unorganised sector.

Banfied, in his study has identified the nature of relationship between the unorganised and organised sectors. His study is worth mentioning in this connection. He has stated that:

"Many small scale operators are engaged in a process of production and of technological development but their ability to develop cumulatively over extended periods is limited by their being exploited through the terms of trade; by their dependence on large scale industry for inputs (after illegally obtained) and by the fact that when the markets they serve grow beyond a certain size this will not be a gradual but accelerating stimulus to further development of the forces of production. Instead, it will trigger a discontinuous shift to international technology which will incorporate this market by virtue of its efficiency and or its market power the latter based on effectively limited, access to capital and on the establishment of brand name products through heavy advertising." [15]

Benfied has stressed the exploitive character of these linkages through the terms of trade and the dependence of unorganised sector on organised sector for inputs.

The inter-dependence of the organised and unorganised sectors is also clear from the fact that sizeable number of establishments in the unorganised sector depend upon the organised sector for marketing of their own products and acquisition of technology on the other hand, as the marketing costs of the unorganised sector remains lower than the organised marketing cost, the unorganised sector is used for marketing goods produced in the organised sector. The large scale producers save the marketing cost through this process. Moreover, the cheap quality commodities such as textiles garments, wood wares, plastic wares, metal wares, leather wares etc., produced by the large scale industries in the organised sector, are sold through small retailers, travelling salesmen or pavement retailers, 'whose activities' are included in the unorganised sector. Similarly, newspapers, magazines and books, published by large establishments are sold by the boys on the streets, and stalls or delivered at houses.

Contrary to the above, a large number of commodities produced in the unorganised sector are marketed by the organised sector at a considerable profit of its own which pay a very low price to the procedures of those commodities in the unorganised sector. The commodities produced by individual craftsmen or traditional workers, who do not have the capacity to reach the consumers directly are sold by the large companies under their brand name. It has been seen that sometimes organised sector marketing agencies charge commission for selling the products, produced in the unorganised sector for the upper class society, in the national and international markets. It is a fact that the poverty and backwardness among the traditional workers in the unorganised sector, is due to the control of markets by a few marketing agencies. This restricts the possibility of technological change or innovation in the production processes of traditional products. The Planning Commission of India commissioned a series of studies on such practices.

Mr. V. B. Singh, Project Director, in the study of 'Chicken Garments' in Lucknow, has stated that:

"The working of the market is such that the producer organisers' surplus has grown while the workers' earning and share in the produce have dwindled...the concentration of riches in the hands of a few and deprivation of the mass of workers both result from the growth of craft taking place in the framework of the market process." [16]

Another form of production linkage is the employment of cheap manual transport facilities for having raw materials or semi-finished industrial goods of large companies, on a piece rate basis. This work is given on a contract basis which remains outside the organised sector. In this manner, most of the work and wage regulations are avoided. In case the same operations are conducted by the organised sector, it would have to be done at much higher wages and on "time rate' basis.

The unorganized and organised sectors relationship is found in those large enterprises or industries where casual labour is employed on a contract basis along with regular workers. The casual labour is paid much less wages and it is deprived from the benefits of employment such as medical facilities, pension benefits, educational facilities to children, etc. This practice is mostly found in those industrial units where the demand for labour varies reasonably.

Casual labour is mostly employed in construction companies, sugar industries and textiles mills. These industries employ casual workers in different categories namely, temporary workers, badli workers, daily workers etc. These workers do not belong to trade unions and do not avail advantages which are enjoyed by the permanent workers. Thus, the attachment of casual labour to the organised manufacturing enterprises is the testimony of linkages of unorganised sector with the organised sector.

It is advantageous for the large establishments to keep the number of workers low on paper so as to reduce the labour costs. The wages of unreported workers is kept low and their daily working hours generally remain above the hours fixed under the relevant regulations. Casual workers are employed as they are not covered by labour laws.

Some of the large establishments split their production processes in different places so that they may be treated as separate small units. The size of each unit is, thus, reduced to keep it outside the factory sector and to avoid the labour regulations. The sick units employ labour on ad-hoc basis and pay wages at piece rate basis.

There is another linkage between the unorganised sector and organised sector. Industrial and household waste is often recycled by the casual labour engaged in scavenging operations. Various types of waste pieces such as metal piece, plastic products, bags, corks, glass and wood pieces etc. are separated and recycled into industrial production at lower cost by women and children. If this operation is conducted by the organised sector, it would have to pay higher wages and may involve large capital outlays.

It has been observed that a large number of companies and corporations sub-contract for parting their activities to small units outside their own establishments. The work outside the organised sector is done at a cheaper rate. There is no other way to reduce the cost of production, in large units, except by way of wage reduction. The National Productivity Council in its study on the wages in mines and plantations has shown the occupational wage disparities in Indian industries. [17]

Examples of sub-contracting in the mechanical engineering industries, electrical and electronic industries, food processing industries, garments, textiles and furniture industries are focused in the studies made by Watanabe (1978) [18] and Papola and Mathur (1980) [19] Chaudhary, T. Datta, has shown linkages between the unorganised and organised sectors in his study. He has shown how the interaction between two sectors determines wage, availability of finance and output of the total economy. [20]

There are also indirect linkages between the organised and unorganised sectors. The traders of fresh vegetables and fruits, labour engaged in construction of buildings and houses and repair services, domestic servants etc. are dependent for their livelihood on the clients whose income is dependent up on the organised sector activities. Thus, the growth of the organised sector's productivity and incomes would create more demand for unorganised sector activities. The researchers have, therefore, concluded that unorganised sector dies and lives with organised sector. [21]

But the rise in the demand for organised sector goods may increase the organised sector production and wages which may reduce the demand for unorganised sector products and services. This may be the adverse effect of growth of organised sector.

The unorganised sector is in no way an independent and exclusive sector. It is linked to, or in many cases, dependent on the organised sector and the rest of the economy through a variety of linkages. It depends on the organised sector for raw materials and other capital requirements, generation of employment, marketing facilities, and so on. The subcontracting model is used by the formal sector for engaging labour in the unorganised sector.

The above discussion clearly reflects that the two sectors are neither exclusive nor have watertight compartments. The unorganised sector is in no way an independent entity. As a matter of fact, unorganised sector is linked to the organised sector in a variety of ways.

End Notes

1. Annual Report, Ministry of Labour, Government of India, p. 20-22.
2. ILO—World Employment Report: Employment in global Economy: How Training Matters," Geneva, 1998-99.
3. Jan Breman, "A Dualistic Labour System?" A Critique of the Unorganised Sector Concept.
4. Sethuraman, S.V., "The Urban Unorganised Sector: Labour Concept, Measurement and Policy," International Labour Review, July-August, 1976, p. 75.
5. King, K., "Kenya's Unorganised Machine Makers: A Study of Small Scale Industry in Kenya's Emergent Artisan Society", World Development, April-May, 1974, p. 20.
6. Souza, P.R. Tokman, E., "The Unorganised Urban Sector in Latin America, ILR, Vol.114, No. 3, November-December, 1975, p. 356.
7. Luball, Harold, "Under Development and Employment in Calcutta," International Labour Review, Vol. 109, No. 1, July,

1973, p. 28.
8. ILO, World Development Programme, 1978, p. 13.
9. Papola, T.S., "Informal Sector: Concept and Policy," E.P.W, Vol. 15, No. 8, 1980, p. 821.
10. John Weeks, "Policies for Extending Employment in the unorganised urban sector of Developing Economics," International Labour Review, January, 1975, p. 3.
11. Heather and Joshi, "Surplus Labour and City," A Study in Bombay, 1976.
12. Papola, T.S., op.cit.
13. Sethuraman, S.V., op.cit, p. 76.
14. Bose, A.N., "The Unorganised Sector in the Calcutta Metropolitan Economy", ILO, Geneva, 1970.
15. Benfied, M., "The Unorganised Sector and Peripheral Capitalism, The Case of Tanzania", Institute of Development Studies Bulletin, Vol. 6, 1975, pp. 53-73.
16. Singh, V.B. et al., "Survey of Urban Handicrafts in U.P. (Chiken), Mrives, p. 4-5, Planning Commission of India, New Delhi, 1976.
17. National Productivity Council, "Occupational Wage Disparities in Mines and Plantations, Memo, NPC, New Delhi, 1977.
18. Watanabe, S., "Technological Linkages between Organised and Unorganised Manufacturing Industries, WEPR Working paper No. 34, ILO, Geneva, 1978.
19. Papola, T.S., and Mathur, R.S., "Inter-sector Linkages in Manufacturing: A Study of Metal Engineering Industry in Kaptur," ILO, Geneva, 1980.
20. Chaudhary, T. Datta, "A Theoretical Analysis of the Unorganised Sector," World Development, Vol. 17, No. 3, 1989, pp. 351-355.
21. Odded Stark, "On Modelling the Unorganised Sector", World Development, Vol. 10, No. 5(1982), pp. 413-441.

4

Growth and Components of the Unorganized Sector

4.1 Unorganized Sector: A Brief History

The unorganised sector is an economic activity that is neither taxed nor monitored by a government; and is also not included in government's Gross National Product (GNP); as opposed to an organized economy.

Though the unorganised economy is often associated with developing countries—where up to 60 percent of the labour force (with as much as 40 percent of GDP) works, yet all economic systems contain an unorganised economy in some proportion.

The rapid growth of urban areas in developing countries in the 1950s and 1960s increased the problem of unemployment. The International Labour Organisation (ILO) sponsored missions to investigate the problem. These missions showed that the employment was growing fast for less rapidly then the growth of population. However, the surplus population to some extent was absorbed in small sector manufacturing concerns and allied activities, which provided a meagre income to the workers. As a matter of fact, the term unorganised sector designates such areas of economic activities which provide casual employment. The general information available on the subject shows that women rather than men are more engaged in this sector.

History of economic development in the world reveals that the women entered the labour market as wage earner after the Industrial Revolution. This Revolution created employment opportunities for women but they occupied secondary work place in the labour market. In developing countries, the participation of working women is not properly recognised.

Statistics on the unorganised economy are unreliable by virtue of the subject, yet they can provide a tentative picture of its relevance: For example, unorganised employment makes up 48 percent of non-agricultural employment in North Africa, 51 percent in Latin America,65 percent in Asia, and 72 percent in sub-Saharan Africa. If agricultural employment is included, the percentage rises, in some countries like India and many sub-Saharan African countries beyond 90 percent. Estimates for developed countries are around 15 percent.

In developing countries, the largest part of unorganised work, around 70 percent, is self-employed, in developed countries, wage employment predominates. The majority of unorganised economy workers are women. Policies and developments affecting the unorganised economy have, thus, a distinctly gendered effect.

4.2 Migration of Rural Labour to Cities

Migration of rural men and women to neighbouring towns and cities has contributed a lot in the development of unorganised sector in the district. In rural areas where women are no longer able to make an important contribution to household economy, they are usually forced to migrate out of rural areas. Moreover, due to inadequate increase in employment opportunities for rural poor, lack of satisfactory increase in agricultural production, natural calamities, inadequate infrastructure facilities, lack of civic amenities etc., have pushed the rural people to migrate to urban areas of the district. In addition, the development of infrastructure, educational facilities and employment opportunities in urban areas of the district have pulled the poor people to migrate to these areas. The survey of the district area has shown that females have more migrated from rural to urban areas as compared to men. The migrated women get jobs in unorganised sectors such as construction work, small-scale industrial units, domestic work etc. but there is hardly any opportunity to improve their earnings.

In the recent past, rural migrants have been adult males with or without families but the traditional pattern in the district has changed with young women now have formed a large proportion of the rural-urban drift. The sex specific migration is mainly due to undermining the domestic activities of rural women. Thus, they migrate from villages to urban centres of the district mainly for the purpose of earning a living. Observations show that these women lack minimum level of skill and education, which is required for the employment in the urban organised sector. As rural women usually do not fulfil those requirements, which are needed for stable employment in organised sector, they are forced into the subsistence economy or the unorganised sector. However, in the district, women migrants have occupied an important place in the unorganised sector.

A backward rural economy in the villages surrounding Bulandshahr city forces the migration of a large section of its population into the urban areas of the district, in search of work. The situation of these migrants is so desperate that they are completed to accept work at very low wages in order to sustain themselves.

4.3 Non-availability of Jobs in Modern Sector

Another factor that has developed the unorganised sector in the district is non-availability of modern sector jobs even to those women and men who live in urban places and have some educational qualification and skill. The employment opportunities in the modern sectors are rare due to technological development in these sectors. These sectors are capital intensive rather than labour intensive.

Thus, a large number of unemployed men and women are attracted by the unorganised sector as entry is easy there and it provides income, though insufficient, to the family. The meagre income that they get is precious for their own and for their families' survival.

4.4 Women in Agricultural Sector

During 1990-91, the contribution of agriculture to the country's GDP output was at 32 percent, which decreased to 20 percent by 2005-06. While the industry and services sectors contributed to 80 percent of the GDP which would increase further, with all of India's big corporate houses focusing on infrastructure and IT segments. The GDP contribution for sector depends on how much investments it can attract from the people, and the overdependence on industrial sectors would mean that India is slowly shifting from an agrarian based economy to that dependant on imports and exports.

The agricultural sector in India is the largest sector in the country's economy. It contributes almost 18.5 percent to India's GDP, while it accounts for about 13 percent of the country's total exports. For the past couple of years (2006-07 and 2007-08), the agriculture and allied sector saw a growth rate of more than 4 percent, comparing to the growth rate of 2.5 percent during the 10th Five Year Plan. Due to the huge market potential, Indian Agricultural Industry has become the home to a number of top agricultural companies.

Agriculture is the main occupation of the people residing in these areas. In the district vast majority of women workers are employed in agriculture sector. Amongst rural women workers about 85 percent are employed in agriculture as labourers. Agriculture labours are those who are engaged in raising crops and allied activities on payment of wages. Survey of the area has revealed that two third of the agriculture operations are performed by women. Thus, agricultural operations in the district are characterized as relatively greater involvement of women than men. Landless women labourers may be classified as (a) permanent workers, (b) seasonal workers and (c) workers when needed.

The women participate in agricultural operations besides the household work. They perform all of the family duties as well. The women labourers play a multi-dimensional role in agriculture and allied sectors and in domestic work.

4.5 Women in Small Industrial Sector

In the district the women workers are employed in small sized manufacturing establishments which are less capital intensive. Though these women perform various types of jobs but they are particularly employed in simple production process.

The small manufacturing units which produce cotton clothes including Khadi ready-made clothes, silk and woollen garments, handicrafts, wooden and brass toys, perfume and scented oils, biscuits, carpets and durries, sarees and ladies dresses have employed women workers in their establishments. These women are paid low wages either on piece rate basis or at weekly or monthly basis. They have been employed temporarily.

The handicraft sector is one of the largest decentralised and unorganised sector of the Indian economy. Handicraft forms second largest employment sector in India after agriculture. There are twenty-three million crafts people in India today.

4.6 Women in Construction Sector

The building and construction sector is employing a large number of workers in the district. The construction work is an important source of absorbing unemployed people because it relies on unskilled labour. This sector is labour intensive sector. Since working women are unskilled, they are involved in those activities of construction work, which invite only manual labour. These women workers are assigned the work of carrying earth, mortar, cement, stores, water, bricks etc. on their heads or backs from the place of storage to the site. They are also absorbed in road construction and repair work, for crushing the stone, carrying the head loads and also for working on hand pumps etc. It is noteworthy that in construction work, the women workers are assigned all sorts of the physically exhaustive tasks.

Construction workers as a whole are included in exploited

category of workers. Women workers within this category are subject to a more intensive form of job insecurity. In this sector, women operate in the capacity of a reserve army. They are drawn upon in situations of excess demand and are retrenched as the demand decreases. Under this sector women have to work without any possibility of promotion or permanency.

There are three main considerations that belong to the employment of women workers in construction work:

1. Women labourers are cheaper than male labourers.
2. Women workers are more disciplined and Submissive than male workers.
3. There are some jobs to which male workers are reluctant to accept.

This sector does not guarantee permanent work since it depends on a number of factors such as volume of construction work, type of work, wage rates etc. Despite these factors, a large number of women in the district contribute in the construction of building, roads, projects etc.

As is clear from the nature of this work it provides intermittent employment of a casual nature to the women workers. The women workers who migrate from rural areas to urban areas of the district are mostly absorbed by the construction work. The job of unskilled women workers is more strenuous in construction work than in other manufacturing industries. Their short duration of employment, frequent movement from one site to another and meagre wages have made it difficult for them to have a settled life. The working conditions of women workers employed in construction work is so deplorable that Padmini Sen Gupta has called these women contract labourers as "women of the desert." [1] These women are drawn from poor classes and the major share of the family's income is their earnings. Thus, these women stand at the lower level of the society.

These are progressive labour laws in India but they are not enforced. The abolition of Contract Labour Act, 1971, sought to eliminate the practice of Contract Labour, provides some benefits such as maternity leave and medical facilities to women labourers. However, it is violated. As a matter of fact, the labourers are unaware of these rights.

The career of women construction workers starts as simple labourers and they remain at the same position till they become unfit for the job. Even the experience of these women is not recognised by the contractors.

Most of the construction workers are out of employment during the monsoons. In quarries and brick kilns as well as big construction sites, a system of bondage exists and gets extended from one generation to the next through child labour. The existing labour laws applicable to construction workers are based on inspection, prosecution, fines etc. However, legal processes are so time consuming that the aggrieved workers may be out of employment or employed elsewhere by the time redressal materializes. He/she cannot leave his/her worksite, forgoing his/her daily wages to go elsewhere to pursue complaints against violation of laws. His/her lot, therefore, is one of near helplessness in the face of injustice and exploitation. The existing laws do not give adequate protection to workers against victimisation.

In the post-liberalisation period, Indian construction industry is witnessing many structural changes which are going to radically transform the industry as well as the construction labour market. Since the industry has so far been based on labour intensive technologies, it has been a source of ready employment to large masses of urban and rural poor.

In fact, one major factor, which has been discouraging the modernisation of the construction industry, is the abundance of cheap labour. The present trend towards induction of modern technology in construction industry is likely to transform the traditional labour market, and indicates that there would be increased mechanisation, and manual and it women workers would, therefore, be increasingly eliminated from large construction projects.

4.7 Domestic Service Sector

Domestic work represents up to 10 percent of total employment in several countries, according to ILO's labour statistics (January 20, 2010). Yet, it is generally undervalued, overworked, underpaid, unprotected and, therefore, open to abuse of children and adults as well. Indeed, a significant proportion of domestic workers are children in spite of international treaties and national laws prohibiting it.

Domestic service is an important occupation for women in Urban and semi-urban areas. This occupation is predominantly filled in by the migrants from the rural areas, surrounding the district. Job opportunities in the domestic service offer rural women the chance of moving to urban areas. During survey of the district area, it was revealed that many rural families allowed their daughters to move to the towns just because there were no jobs in the domestic services in which the basic minimum needs of the young women i.e. food and clothes were of covered. It has also been seen that parents feel their young daughters more secured if they live with families in town. It is a fact that most make the more willingly; some are brought or sent and a few are brought against their wishes.

Employers of the women domestic servants are mainly the businessmen, doctors, teacher, government employees and other high economic strata families. The women domestic servants, on the basis of their contract with their employers can be classified as (i) full time workers, (ii) part time workers, and (iii) residential workers. The full time workers are attached with a simple household for the whole day. The residential workers live in the families as family members doing all types of household works. The part time domestic servants are the workers who make themselves available for households' works for a short duration every day. They serve a number of houses for duration of 1-3 hours a day.

The jobs assigned to women domestic servants at all the places and for all types of maids is almost the same. They are given the jobs such as cooking, cleaning utensils, washing clothes, sweeping and cleaning the houses, fetching water, bringing vegetables and provisions, looking after children etc. The caste factor is considered in case of working as higher caste employers do not allow scheduled caste women in cooking.

The wages paid to these working women are determined by the nature of job or, of their work. The wages given for manual household's services are lower than that offered for manual works such as escorting the children to school, looking after children etc. The residential workers get lower wages in cash than that earned by the non-residential. In addition to the monthly wages, the residential maids are provided food and shelter by the employers. During the questionnaire, the residential maids had told that the quality of food given to them was not the same as what their employers ate.

The demand for women domestic servants however, is not uniform all throughout the year. In urban areas of the district the demand for part time domestic servants increases during the period of winter.

The employers' attitude towards the female servants has changed in recent years. Apart from the wages, these servants are given new clothes and festival grants in cash. Sometimes the children of the servants' families are also given some gifts. Annual increments in wages are also granted to part time and full time domestic servants. These women domestic servants serve the particular households for years who give some incentives.

In spite of such positive attitude of a number of employers, the women workers have some genuine grievances against the housewives. A few of the upper strata housewives when contacted insisted that they treated their maid servants just like members of their families but upon questioning the maid servants of the houses, they explained the story of their exploitation at the hands of the employers.

There are several employers in Bulandshahr city who consider maid servants as invisible objects generally to be ignored. They feel that servants should not be allowed to move freely inside the house, they should be under strict vigilance all the times and there is no need for maid servants to be educated and so on.

The performance of domestic workers by means of paid domestic service from women has many notable consequences. The availability of cheap domestic services affects the quality of life of the middle and upper middle strata enjoying such services. If domestic services were not available, these services would then have to be purchased from established enterprises such as restaurants, laundry, dry cleaning shops etc., at higher prices. In some cases the employment of domestic maid help frees the housewife from many of her domestic obligations. Housewives, only occasionally supervise their work. The employment of domestic maid might encourage house women to take full time jobs in the organised or unorganised sectors. Furthermore, such employment of maids may encourage housewife to have a life of leisure and comfort.

The study of female domestic servants in Lima, Peru, conducted by Margo Smith has reflected that "Domestic service provides one of the few opportunities available to lower class migrant women for upward socio-economic mobility within the broad spectrum of the lower classes." [2]

The remuneration paid to women sometimes includes the labour of daughters. Thus, young girls work as a components of their 'mothers' wage. The task that the women domestic labourers is required to do are often divided between mother and daughter. More responsibility is, however, placed on the daughter but she does not receive the cash in payment. During the survey of the study area, it was found in many cases that the mother labourer goes to serve as domestic labour earlier, leaving her daughter to finish the work. The mother receives one meal a day, one dhoti a year, and ₹ 400 (average) a month while daughter gets two meals a day and clothes once a year but no cash. The kind consideration given to daughter reduces the cost of living of domestic women workers.

4.8 Self-employed Sector

In India, self-employment opportunities have considerable relevance. Self employment is regarded as one of the important profitable area challenging enterprises among the various unorganised sector occupations.

In Bulandshahar district, a large number of women, especially in the urban and semi-urban areas are self employed. Most of them are street vendors and petty business women. A low capital is involved in it.

Artisan women are also absorbed in self employment activities such as handicrafts producers and household enterprises like knitting and weaving etc.

As a matter of fact, self employed women are those who have full control on products and the market. These women are the owners of their means of production. They do not work for an employer. They have several customers of their own. The rate of the products is fixed by themselves keeping in view the volume of the work and the market competition. Thus, self-employed workers may be said as own account workers.

There are piece-rate workers also in the district. There is a distinction between self employed workers own-account workers and piece rate workers. The own account workers work at their own place and set their own level of production. The level of production, however, depends upon the amount of money they have, extent of raw material they can purchase, number of family members, their contact with the purchasers in the market and the demand for their goods. The self employed women workers take their own risks.

The piece rate workers, on the other hand, are skilled in their own occupations. They do only this kind of work but women workers among them are exploited as they have no other choice to earn money for their survival. These workers have no other identity except that they are mere workers. But in case of self employed unorganised sector, one person has multiple roles as worker, employer and owner.

In the urban areas of the district, women run roadside tea

and water stalls and vegetables and fruit shops. They are also engaged in street vending retailing in cotton and woollen garments, second-hand clothes, utensils etc.

A large number of women petty grocers are also found in the district. The women also work as dry cleaners, pressers, washers, tailors, porters and clay work retail traders.

In the urban areas of the district women are running a number of beauty parlours mainly in cities such as Bulandshahr, Khurja, Sikandrabad, Anupshahr and Dibai etc. All these women have been included in the self employment category as they are considered as petty traders.

A question that arises here is whether petty traders' activities should be included in the preview of unorganised sector? These traders possess a stall in the market or at a fixed place on the street and also pay the required rent and taxes to the local administration. In view of these facts, it may be argued that these workers do not fall in the category of unorganised sector. But this opinion does not hold good as these works do not fulfil various other requirements as are needed to include them in the organised sector. There is no entrance barrier for the workers in these traders, no minimum education or skill is required, their work conditions are not regulated, they are not covered by any social security benefits and thus, petty traders' activities cannot be included in the organised sector.

It is a fact that the self employed women workers are a major part of the unorganised sector in the district. The self-employed poor women mostly belonging to scheduled and backward castes are engaged in street vending. Street vending activity has no barriers with respect to access because the street provides free open space for them. They also sell their goods from door to door in colonies. Vending in the streets requires very small capital.

The condition of women petty traders is also bad. It is almost the same as of women street vendors. The women petty traders collect capital from unorganised credit markets at higher rate of interest. Thus, petty women traders have higher capital cost than that of the street vendors. As women petty traders are powerless, they are victimized by the police and they suffer from constant intimidation by market inspectors. Thus, a very dismal picture of women petty traders was noticed during the survey of the study area. It reveals that petty trade is not a promising unorganised sector activity.

The women hawkers on the streets of the urban and semi-urban residential areas, selling flowers, vegetables, fruits, ready food items etc. are very prominent. These hawkers are confined to the lowest range of the trading hierarchy. It was found during survey that they are in debt to money-lenders or to wholesale suppliers. Thus, they spend much of their earning in payment of exorbitant weekly interest charges.

It is true that women are encouraged by these ventures as they do not require much capital. As these ventures are labour intensive, the male members of the family extend necessary help to the female workers. The women, thus, find petty trade as the best suitable way to utilise idle time to increase family income.

It was found during survey that most of women petty traders have established their shops or stalls mainly at their residences or at the nearby market places. Thus, they do not feel separation between workplace and domestic place. Due to this fact, the degree of tension to women petty traders is somewhat less than that faced by women workers in other unorganised sectors such as construction works domestic services etc.

It has been observed that the rural women are mainly engaged in dealing with vegetables, grocery items, fruits, readymade food items whereas the urban women are retailing cotton and woollen garments, second-hand clothes, utensils etc. and are running roadside food, tea and water stalls. The women migrated from rural areas of the district are mostly street vendors and hawkers selling various consumable items. It has been noticed that while a section of women petty traders are relatively higher income earners other are found to be the mere subsistence earners.

Thus, unorganised sector has a crucial role in our economy in terms of employment and its contribution to the National Domestic Product, savings and capital formation. At present, Indian economy is passing through a process of economic reforms and liberalization. During the process, merger, integration of various firms within the industry and up gradation of technology and other innovative measures take place to enhance competitiveness of the output both in terms of cost and qualitative to compete in the international market.

Inefficient units either wither away or merge with other ones performing better. In this situation, there is a special need to take care of the interests of the workers by providing them training, upgrading their skills, and other measures to enable them to find new avenue of employment, improve their productivity in the existing employment, necessary to enhance the competitiveness of their product both in terms of quality and cost which would also help in improving their income and thereby raising their socio economic status. It has been experienced that formal sector could not provide adequate opportunities to accommodate the workforce in the country and unorganised sector has been providing employment for their subsistence and survival. Keeping in view the existing economic scenario, the unorganised sector will expand further in the years to come. Thus, it needs to be strengthened and activated so that it could act as a vehicle of employment provider and social development.

End Notes

1. Padmini, Sen Gupta, "Women Workers in India", Asia Publishing House, Bombay, 1960, p. 185.
2. Margo, L. Smith, "Domestic Service as a Channel of Upwards Mobility for the Lower Class Women: The Lima Case." Female and Male in Latin America, Percatello (ed.), Pittsburgh, University of Pittsburgh, 1973.

5

Problems of Unorganized Women Workers

The unorganised sector is characterized by the several factors such as wage discrimination, no limit for minimum wages, long hours of work, lack of jobs security, lack of legislative cover, lack of minimum facilities at work place, heavy physical work, and ill treatment, sexual harassment and exploitation by the employers. These factors with regard to women workers are discussed below.

5.1 Wage Discrimination

Statement by US Secretary of Labour Hilda L. Solis on Equal Pay Day (20-4-2010) Washington, "Nearly a half century after the Equal Pay Act was enacted to ensure equal pay for equal work, this form of discrimination continues to impinge upon women's rights in the workplace."

Most women work whether, they are paid or unpaid. Women do a lot of unpaid work within the household, in family farms and enterprises. Despite its obvious economic and social worth, much of the work that women do remains 'invisible' in national accounting and censuses and even while defining the 'informal sector' and assessing its contribution to the GDP.

Estimates based on the National Sample Survey (NSS) 1999-2000, women are said to account for one-third, about 400 million, of the unorganised sector workers in India. These figures would be much larger if the unpaid work done by most women is recognized and included, even then, they have not been considered equal to man in practice from the ancient times. It is a fact that discrimination against women is widely prevalent in India. Despite their contribution in primary sector, they are not viewed as being within the productive system. Most of the women work in unorganised sector for low wages because of illiteracy, ignorance, low level of skills etc., and these factors hamper them to bargain for increase in wages. Women workers are paid much less in comparison to men for doing the same work. They are also discriminated in entering into gainful employment in public and private sectors.

The Mona Foundation's Barli Development Institute for Rural Women, Indore said that "India is working to change that problem." The Institute provides education to young women in India in order to help them develop practical skills like reading, sewing, and horticulture—and more abstract ones like confidence and self esteem—they need in order to start businesses, produce food, care for their families, and improve their Livelihoods.

In agriculture, greater involvement of women than the men is found. During survey of the study area, the women workers reported differential wage distribution in agriculture sector. It is also observed that in agriculture labour of both men and women is of the same quality but they do not earn equal wages in farm operations.

5.2 Greater Involvement of Rural Women in Agriculture

In small industrial units also women workers are paid lesser wages than the male workers for the same work. The producers mostly engage women workers for such jobs as it reduces the cost of production.

Women construction workers are also target of wage discrimination in this district, although the women construction workers undertake the same hard work done by men workers like crushing the stone, carrying the clay and mortars through the readymade staircases leading to multi-storeyed buildings etc., they are paid much less than the payment made to male workers. For example, in Bulandshahr district, a man engaged in crushing stones is paid wages between ₹ 100 to ₹ 120 per day, depending upon the age and efficiency, while a women is paid only between ₹ 70 to ₹ 90 per day for the same work. The wage discrimination aspect has created a feeling of desperation among the women workers.

Ravindra Nath Tagore, a great Indian poet, had expressed the inequality of the situation in the following words: "O Lord why have you not given woman the right to conquer her destiny? Why does she have to wait head bowed, by the road side, waiting with tired patience, hoping for a miracle in the morrow?" [1]

The women domestic servants are also discriminated in the matter of wage payment. Women workers are paid relatively much less wages than their male counterparts. In survey of the study area, it was found that full time male domestic servants were paid ₹ 2500 to ₹ 3000 per month while the full time female domestic servants were paid ₹ 1500 to ₹ 2000 per month.

5.3 Equal Pay: A Matter of Survival

America first put an equal-pay law on the books in 1963, when women earned 59 cents for every dollar earned by a man. While this legislation was landmark at the time, its core provisions require updating if it is to fulfil its promise. Nearly 50 years later, the wage gap has narrowed by only 18 cents. Despite news reports that the gap narrowed in the last year, the census report released this week showed otherwise. Working women are still paid only 77 cents for every dollar earned by a man—and are paid less than men even when they have similar levels of experience and education. For women of colour, the gap is larger (The Miami Herald, 2010).

Thus, the wage discrimination is found in the entire unorganised sector as women are regarded inferior to men in every respect. However, their family and social circumstances compel them to work on much lower wages in the unorganised sector.

The need of the hour is to support in whichever way possible and to stop discrimination, violence and atrocities being committed against women. There is a need to recognize the immense contribution that the women are making to our agricultural economy. These steps are mandatory for the freedom and establishment of equal rights and opportunities for rural women.

5.4 No Limit for Minimum Wages

In agriculture sector, the wages vary from women to women and from place to place. Thus, the women agricultural labourers in the district earn differential wages by negotiating contacts with the land owners. Their wages are low and they are denied all human considerations. In agriculture sector, there is no limit for minimum wages. They are usually paid less on the ground of being less productive and they always remain at the mercy of landlords.

In small manufacturing units, women are employed generally by the contractors and sub-contractors. The names of these women workers are not shown in the muster roll and thus, they are not treated as regular employees. As a result of this, they are not given wages and other benefits which the regular employees avail as per labour legislation. The women piece rate workers mostly work in their houses. They usually work under contractors. The contractor supply raw material to them and take finished goods. Thus, they are not covered under the Minimum Wages Act and Factories Act. These women workers lodged complaints about short payment and unexplained deductions.

The construction workers are covered by the Minimum wages Act, but this Act has never been implemented in our study area. In the district, though the government is also employer in construction sector for many construction projects such as roads, bridges, government buildings etc., yet the public works are constructed on contract basis. The construction contractors seek the services of labour contractors for supplying labour at the construction site. The labour contractors receive commission from the construction contractors for supplying the workers. The commission paid to the labour contractor is deducted from the wages paid to labourers. The abolition of Contract Labour Act, 1971 was promulgated to eliminate the practice of contract labour and to provide some benefits such as maternity leave and some medical facilities to women workers. However, the provisions of this Act are violated in practice. It is a fact that labourers are also not aware of their rights. Thus, the women workers in construction sector accept lower wages due to the fear of losing the employment if they insist for higher wages.

In domestic service too, there is no minimum limit for wages. In the study area, the wages of female domestic servants are determined on the basis of their contract with the employers depending upon the nature of jobs assigned to them. For domestic servants, minimum wages is an alien work. The wage of such women workers are not determined by any criteria. The wages for the same quantum of work varies from one household to the other. Thus, in the domestic sector, women workers are exposed to acute poverty. It can perhaps be said without fear of contradiction, that a large majority, perhaps a predominant majority of those engaged in this category of service are women and children. An estimate made by the College of Social Work in Bombay claims that 80 percent of domestic workers are women.

Domestic work in the cities is seen as one avenue of employment by poor women from both rural and suburban areas. These women who work as domestic labour are part of an exploitative informal economy where they work without formal contracts, work benefits or social protection employed by formal or informal enterprises/employers or by households and fall within the category of informal wage employment. The globalisation has opened avenues for women in the informal sector, 'low wages, insecurities and complete lack of organisational strength have characterised the quality of their employment.' At the micro level it is the vicissitudes of an insecure family life which drives women to take up domestic work as a form of employment. Since domestic work is not a 'skilled' job, it is an avenue of employment of poor, largely illiterate and semi-literate women, and they continue to persist in domestic work even though they are without substantial rights and benefits. Domestic workers in our country are not organised, and a relative degree of economic freedom does not ensure them their rights.

5.5 Long Hours of Work

For most women living in rural and remote parts of India, the day begins as early as 3:00 am. The flour for the day's meals needs grinding, livestock need to be fed, breakfast needs to be cooked, and water needs to be carried from wells, rivers, and streams. And that's all before the children—usually just the boys— head off to school for the day. In general, in rural India women work more and sleep less than their male counterparts. And they have almost no access to education.

In unorganised sector the hours of work are longer than permitted by law and no payment for overtime is made to the workers. Moreover, women put more hours of work than men but they earn much less than the men.

In short, while women have begun to take on new roles in the workforce, once dominated by men, men have not taken on new roles in the household, still dominated, therefore, by women.

In agriculture sector, women typically work more hours of work per day than men. During survey agricultural women workers reported that in ordinary days, they perform agricultural operations and allied activitics 7 to 8 hours a day. In addition, they also spend 6 to 8 hours in household activities. They also said that in the peak season, they spend 9 to 10 hours per day on farm activities. It has, therefore, been said that "A man may work from sun to sun but a woman's work never done."

Rural women form the backbone of the agricultural labour force across much of the developing world. Globally, more than a third of the female workforce is engaged in agriculture.

In factories and small-scale industrial units women work for longer hours but they are not paid for the extra hours devoted by them for work.

"Women and young girls have to allocate large amounts of time to the collection of firewood, compounding gender inequalities in livelihood opportunities and education. Collecting fuel wood and animal dung is a time-consuming and exhausting task, with average loads often in excess of 20 kg. Research has found that rural women in some areas o f the district walk 5-10 kilometres a day collecting and carrying firewood, with loads averaging 15 kg. to 20 kg.

That' why, it is observed that in rural India, average collection times can amount to over 3 hours a day. Beyond the immediate burden on time and body, fuel wood collection often results in young girls being kept out of school."

Women domestic workers who live in the families as residential workers serve the families round the clock. Full time domestic women workers work 10 to 12 hours a day.

5.6 Lack of Health Facilities at Work Place

Minimum facilities to workers at work place are not provided in the unorganised sector.

In agriculture sector, women work under miserable conditions. They are not provided minimum facilities at the workplace. Their working conditions in fields are very poor in terms of their hard labour. It is a fact that they work in such situations, which are not bearable.

The manufacturing small-scale industries which employ women as casual labour provide unsatisfactory physical environment and surroundings at the place of work. The place of work generally lacks sufficient light, ventilation, pure water, separate toilets for women and men, proper sitting arrangements, cleanliness and required temperature and humidity etc. Thus, they are derived of minimum facilities of work at work places. Due to unhygienic conditions of work-

workers are exposed to several health hazards.

The working conditions of women workers engaged in construction work are deplorable. These women trudge along hot country roads with babies or their arms on tied on their backs and a bundle of scanty food on their heads. Their hairs become white with dust and their faces are streaked with sweet. During survey of the study area, the common problem expressed by almost all the construction women workers was the lack of privacy on the work spot.

The government regulations provide for amenities at work place such as crèches, sanitary services etc. But unfortunately, these facilities are not provided to women labourers. The working mothers are, therefore, compelled to leave their children uncared for at home. The women construction workers neither receive any accidental, medical or maternity benefits from their employers. Thus, there is a complete denial of welfare measures for these women workers.

Most of the home based working women work under miserable conditions. These women work at their homes mostly situated in slum areas with open drains and no municipal amenities. These women accept work at home on piece rate basis to earn their livelihood.

The domestic women workers are also not provided minimum required facilities for their work. Rural women and girls who become domestics in families of their own communities are no more than slaves while at work.

Rural women are also disadvantaged in their access to health. For instance, in many countries, reproductive health care remains inadequate, and maternal mortality continues to be high, with the highest rates in Sub-Saharan Africa. In every region of the world, the presence of skilled birth attendants is lower in rural than in urban areas.

Most pregnant women in rural areas continue to work while pregnant and resume work soon after delivery. Moreover, the absence of timely medical care, inadequate diet and heavy workload often results in complicated pregnancies and high maternal mortality rates.

The most productive years of a woman's life are the reproductive years. The absence of maternity entitlements often means that a woman worker has to leave her job to have a child. With the near absence of any effective primary health care system in the country, most women are forced to have children at home without any medical care. Majority of the women and their families are unable to bear the burden of hospitalization costs. Even when they opt for hospitalization, additional medical expenses and loss of employment makes women economically vulnerable. Absence of maternity entitlements also means that a woman is unable to take care of her nutritional needs before and after the pregnancy and get adequate rest, and is compelled to start working soon after child birth.

Maternity entitlements are available to all women, whether employed or not, in terms of hospital and medical expenses. These maternity entitlements include paid maternity leave of at least 12 weeks.

Women workers must be paid for the leave as per the living wages they are entitled to. There must be provisions for financial support during childbirth so as to protect the health of mother.

The absence of child care provisions means that the burden of work on women is increased further tremendously, affecting their health and work participation.

A demand for social security for the unorganised sector workers must include childcare provisions from the point of view of women workers. Provisions aimed at ensuring protection and promotion of nutritional needs of mother and child must be included such as time breaks for nursing once the mother rejoins work.

For women workers, their own health and ability to work is usually the only resource they can fall back upon. They are the most vulnerable in this regard because their health and nutrition needs form the least priority within the family.

Women in the poorest households are the least likely to receive medical attention.

5.7 Lack of Job Security

As the nature of employment of women workers employed in unorganised sector is casual or on daily wages or at piece rate, there is no job security for them. Almost all women in this sector face insecurity of jobs. Women working as domestic servants, sweepers, scavengers etc., face insecurity of jobs extremely. In some cases women generally loss jobs for about to six months in a year. Job insecurity is faced by women workers in sectors such as agriculture, small manufacturing units, construction work, domestic services etc. Self employed women, who are part-time workers also loss jobs for a few months in a year.

Insecurity of employment is a major vulnerability that most women face. They are usually the last to be hired and the first to be fired. They are often employed in work which is seasonal in nature. They are predominant in sectors where there is steady loss of employment without a corresponding creation of new avenues for work due to factors such as technological changes, coming in of big domestic and multinational companies, increased imports, forced displacement and government policies. Guarantee of employment and yearlong availability of work is the most basic social security need for women.

Women workers are not guaranteed year long employment. Unemployment benefits are to be made available to all workers equally irrespective of the employment status of any other family member.

5.8 Lack of Legislative Cover

There are no rules and regulations in the unorganised sector. Even the legal rights are ignored. The decentralisation of work is done by small manufacturing units with a view to escape government legislation. The domestic woman workers do not have any legal terms and conditions of employment. These women workers do not get any sort of protection. Agriculture women workers also do not have legal protection in practice. The migrant women workers work in unorganised sector without legal protection. Women construction workers have also been deprived from legislation cover. No protection is provided to these women from the atrocities of the contractors or sub-contractors.

5.9 Heavy Physical Work

Women working in unorganised sectors face complicated situations as they play dual roles and perform dual responsibilities of work place and of their families. These roles result in heavy workload on the working women.

Most of women workers in agriculture sector are given heavy physical work, which they do from early morning till late evening. The entire family work is also their responsibility. In small manufacturing units, women workers, in some cases, are assigned tough physical work as women labour is cheap. This keeps the cost of production of their products cheaper. In construction work the work of crushing stones and carrying the heavy loads are difficult physical work but these tasks are solely assigned to women workers. Domestic women workers are also given all types of manual jobs. Besides other heavy physical jobs, they are also engaged in clearing sewers but they are not equipped with protective overall masks.

'It is a hard fact that employment of women in agriculture sector, construction work and domestic work is not an employment but a coolie work.'

5.10 Exploitation, Sexual Harassment and Ill Treatment

In the district, big farmers exploit scheduled caste and backward caste women workers. Several cases of rebuking, cheating, ill treatment, threatening and beating were reported by agricultural women workers. A few cases of sexual harassment were also brought to notice during survey of the area.

In small manufacturing units, construction work and domestic services women are exploited by employers, contractors and middlemen. Though the problem of sexual harassment is not wide spread in these sectors, however, a few cases of this nature in case of employed girls and young women were reported during survey. The problem of ill treatment is very common in all these sectors.

The self-employed hawkering and vendoring women in urban areas are harassed by police personnel and municipal authorities. A few cases of physical torturing were also reported by the women workers.

In construction work women workers are exploited by exposing themselves to various risks and health hazards. The women domestic workers also suffer from ill treatment by the housewives and other female members of the family.

Sexual harassment and violence at the workplace is a threat faced by all women workers. A demand for social security for the unorganised sector workers must ensure that complaint and redressal mechanisms against sexual harassment at workplace following the Vishakha guidelines are put in place, keeping in mind the specific concerns of women workers in the unorganised sector. The employment security of a female worker must be guaranteed.

Thus, in the unorganised sector, the women workers are tortured physically, economically, socially and emotionally.

The Hon'ble Supreme Court of India in 1997 defined the term sexual harassment. The sexual harassment includes physical contact and advances, sexual favours, sexually coloured remarks, showing of pornography and any other Verbal or non-verbal conduct of sexual nature that is unwelcome and humiliating to the women. The court puts the onus on the employers to provide a safe working environment for their employees. [2]

However, in unorganised sector, the employers do not

provide protection to working women. It was reported that even they themselves indulge in sexual harassment of women working with them.

5.11 Lack of Safe Working Places

For young girls and women coolies who work in unorganized sectors under hazardous conditions like building constructions, bricklins, agriculture fields, small cottage industries, truck loading and unloading, road side micro business, house and stall maids etc. have no security at their work spots.

Good Shepherd Organization (GOSON) established in provides identity cards through a committed social worker with photos to the above category, by which they can get life security fund, daughter's marriage allowance, delivery (child birth) allowance etc. from the Ministry of Labour. Presently, there are about three thousand members are availing benefit of this project.

There is no security for the lives of women in unorganized women sector. They are forced to work under odd and unsafe working places.

In developing countries, 25 percent of rural children do not attend primary schools, compared to 16 percent of urban children and gender inequalities in access to education remain: 69 percent of rural girls compared to 73 percent of rural boys.

Different factors, including the need for their labour, the low levels of education of their parents, and lack of access to quality schooling, account for the high proportion of out-of-school children in rural areas. The gender disparity is partly due to the fact that girls are heavily relied upon for housework and child care.

Other factors that account for girls' unequal access to education in rural areas include a lack of a safe means of transportation, poor security in schools, and the lack of separate sanitation facilities.

5.12 Lack of Landownership for Rural Women

Rural women are particularly vulnerable to poverty. According to the World Bank, 75 percent of the poor in developing countries live in rural areas. While women work on the land, they often do not hold formal and clear land titles. Less than two percent of land in the developing world is owned by women, according to the International Fund for Agricultural Development (IFAD). A lack of rights over land makes women extremely vulnerable to eviction and negatively affects their economic options.

Women's access to credit is also limited because land is the major asset used as collateral to obtain loans. Women have to rely heavily on the unregulated, informal sector to meet their needs, and often pay higher interest rates as a result. While limited access to land and credit affects rural women as a whole, some groups are particularly vulnerable and marginalized, such as widows, indigenous women and women heading households–a growing category, due to male out-migration.

To increase the prosperity and enhance the well-being of rural women, IFAD, another lead UN agency dedicated to gender sensitive rural development, works to strengthen women's leadership and decision-making in agriculture and natural resource management at all levels; advocate in favour of increased investments for rural women in the context of sustainable agricultural development and food security; and invest in technology development and strengthen capacity for gender equality and rural women's empowerment through its grants programme. In general, women are not land or property owners.

A demand for social security for the unorganised sector workers must ensure that: benefits are not tied to land or property. All housing schemes under social security provisions should ensure that titles are in women's name or are in joint names.

Depending solely on contribution based, social insurance

types of schemes to provide old age, disability pensions will be disadvantageous for women because most women are engaged in either unpaid or low paying jobs. Most women also have many interruptions in their working life due to child birth and domestic work at home. Their capacity to contribute to such schemes that too on a regular basis is low.

5.13 Lack of Social Security

In India, women constitute almost half of the total workforce. However, over 96 percent of women work in the informal, unorganised sector. Overall, the informal sector constitutes 93 percent of the workforce of the population of India. Moreover, these workers contribute 62 percent to the gross domestic product (GDP), and 50 percent to the national income. This sector includes workers employed in a wide range of economic activities, from street vendors and casual workers in a tea-shop to agricultural workers, small and marginal farmers to 'bidi' workers, construction workers, salt pan workers and sub-contracted and temporary workers of factories. However, unlike workers in the formal sectors, they do not have access to regular incomes or welfare benefits, making them extremely vulnerable to change and insecurity.

The non-existence of social security provisions for the unorganised workers therefore means that an extremely large section of women in the country remain unprotected. None of the Bills concerned with the unorganised sector workers that are in circulation take unpaid women workers into account.

1. Unpaid women workers are recognized as unorganised sector workers.
2. Women workers, whether paid or unpaid should be eligible for social security entitlements.
3. Social security is available to the unpaid women workers equally.

A demand for social security for the unorganised sector workers must ensure that all categories of women workers are included in the definition of unorganised sector worker, including unpaid workers, domestic workers, sex workers, entertainment workers, migrant workers—seasonal and permanent, street vendors, pre-agricultural and hunter gatherer communities.

All women should be entitled to social security benefits as independent citizens and not as dependents on male earning members or as part of the family/household.

A demand for social security for the unorganised sector workers must ensure that:

1. Employment status of a male member in the family must not be the criterion for availability of the entitlements to women.
2. Women are not treated as dependents on male family members and it is assumed that they are automatically covered by social security coverage.
3. Every woman must have a workers identity card in her own name.
4. Social security provisions must accrue to women as individuals.

Many women workers retire from paid work at an early age, due ill health or simply because they stop getting employment. The absence of old age security provisions would imply leaving them unprotected.

A demand for social security for the unorganised sector workers must include a demand for:

1. Providing adequate pension to retired women workers, widows and single women and should have provisions for old age support.
2. The amount of pension must be based on living wages which accrue to the worker.

Women workers usually find themselves excluded from participation in decision making regarding the administration and implementation of labour laws, even when there is provision for equal participation of workers and employers.

A demand for social security for the unorganised sector workers must ensure that women workers are involved adequately and proportionally at all stages including the drafting, administration and implementation of this Bill. Mechanisms for grievance redressal must be women friendly.

Programme on Women's Economic Social and Culture Rights (PWESCR) Slogan on Social Security!

"Hum mahilayen karti hain adhik kaam, Par hamare shram ki nahin koi pehchaan...Mahilayen mange adhikar aur sammaan, Sampoorna suraksha sarkaar kare pradaan."

(We women do more work, but our work is never acknowledged. Women demand their rights and dignity and the government should provide them with comprehensive social security.)

The National Social Security Board constituted in the Ministry of Labour and Employment made recommendations for providing basic minimum social security cover in the form of life and disability insurance, health and maternity benefit and old age pension to all unorganised workers/occupational groups in a phased manner.

As a follow up, the Rashtriya Swasthya Bima Yojana (RSBY) has been extended to building and other construction workers, licensed railway porters, vendors and hawkers, who are from the unorganised sector and are socially challenged and street vendors. The Government is planning to extend the scheme to such Mahatma Gandhi National Rural Employment Guarantee Scheme (MGNREGS) workers who have completed 15 days or more work during previous financial year, beedi workers and also to unorganized sector workers in hazardous mining and associated industries like slate and slate pencil, dolomite, mica and asbestos etc. The Government has constituted Task Force for suggesting social security schemes for: (i) domestic workers, (ii) street vendors, rickshaw pullers, auto rickshaw/taxi drivers and rag pickers, and (iii) sanitation workers and leather workers. The Task Force for Domestic workers in its first report has recommended extension of health insurance scheme, namely, Rashtriya Swasthya Bima Yojana (RSBY) to domestic workers in the first phase. The proposal is under consideration of the Government.

This information was given by Shri Mallikarjun Kharge, Minister for Labour and Employment in a written reply to a question in the Lok Sabha today (March 15, 2011).

The Unorganised Workers Social Security Act, 2008 has been notified in the Gazette and the Unorganised Workers Social Security Rules, 2009 under the Act have been framed and notified. The Act has since been enforced with effect from 16th May, 2009.

End Notes

1. Tagore, Rabindra Nath, "Women's Lot on East and West", Modern Review, November 1912.
2. Pail and Agrawal, Sunday, Times of India, 24th August, 1997, p. 19.

6

Policies and Programmes for Unorganized Sector Women Workers

6.1 Labour Laws for Women

It is a fact that right from the days of Independence, principles of gender equality and protection of women's rights have been the prime concerns in Indian thinking.

Articles 43 of the Constitution says, "The State shall endow to secure by suitable legislation or economic organisation or any other way to all workers, agricultural, industrial or otherwise work, a living wage, ensuring a decent standard of life and full enjoyment of leisure and social and cultural opportunities."

In view of the aforesaid article of the Constitution, special laws have been enacted for the protection of women workers in factories, mines, plantation etc. In the early phase of country's planning, the concept of women development envisaged as welfare oriented. But later on women were recognized as participants of development. The concept of women development has further changed. Now, the planning has marked a shift from development to 'employment of women'. This change has emphasized that the women must be enable to function as equal partners in the country's development process.

Undoubtedly, labour laws for women workers in India are amongst the most progressive in the world. But the economic, social and physical exploitation of women workers continues. Though the Central and State governments have framed various rules and enacted legislation to combat exploitation but there has been a wide gap between framing rules, enacting legislation and their effective implementation. There are very strict laws for the protection of benefits of working women, which provide safety measures and regulations for working hours and conditions of work and welfare of women workers. But even these rules and regulations have not been able to safeguard the interest of working women in agricultural works, small and household industries, construction work, domestic services and self 'employed sector.' The condition in these sectors is rather worse. Women workers under the adverse circumstances have to do strenuous work at very low wages and inhuman conditions of work without permanency of jobs.

Integrated development of rural areas is one of the abiding tasks before the Government of India. The National Common Minimum Programme (NCMP) of the Central government reiterates the cardinal importance of villages to the overall development of the country and commits to work towards development of rural areas, which for various reasons could not keep pace with urban areas in the past.

In conformity with this commitment of the Government, the Ministry of Rural Development accords foremost priority to development in rural areas and eradication of poverty and hunger from the face of rural India. A number of initiatives have been taken in the recent years for creation of social and economic infrastructure in rural areas to bridge the rural-urban divide as well as to provide food security and fulfil other basic needs of the rural populace.

The renewed emphasis on rural development is also visible in the commensurate progressive increase in the allocation of resources for implementation of poverty alleviation programmes. For the Tenth Five Year Plan, the allocation of funds for rural development programmes has been enhanced to ₹ 76,774 crore as against ₹ 42,874 crore in Ninth Plan.

The government is committed to the task of carrying forward the process by labour reforms, which include women workers in the informal sector.

"The main focus of the policies of the government with regard to women labour has been to remove the handicap under which they work to strengthen the bargaining capacity, to improve their wages and working conditions to enhance their skills and to open up better employment opportunities for them." [1]

Apart from the Factories Act, 1948, the Minimum wages Act, 1948, the Employees Insurance Act, 1948 and the Payment of Bonus Act, 1965, the following Acts have been specifically enacted to protect the interest of working women:

1. The Maternity Benefits Act, 1961, and
2. The Equal Remuneration Act, 1976.

The Maternity Benefits Act regulates the employment of women in certain establishments for a certain period before and after child birth and maternity and other benefits. The Act applies to mines, factories, circus, industry, plantation, shops and establishments employing ten or more persons, except employees covered under the Employees State Insurance Act, 1948. The State Governments can extend it to other establishments.

The Equal Remuneration Act provides for the payment of equal remuneration to men and women workers for the same and similar nature of work. The Act also prohibits any gender discrimination in recruitment and service conditions. Under the Act, the State government has set up a committee to advise the government on providing increasing employment opportunities for women and reviewing the steps taken for effective implementation of the Equal Remuneration Act, 1976.

The Government of India and the Uttar Pradesh government have started various programmes and schemes for the employment of men and women workers.

6.2 National Rural Employment Guarantee Act

Implemented by the Ministry of Rural Development, National Rural Employment Guarantee Act (NREGA) now known as mahatma Gandhi National Rural Employment Guarantee Act (MGNREGA) is the flagship programme of the Government that directly touches lives of the poor and promotes inclusive growth. The Act aims at enhancing livelihood security of households in rural areas of the country by providing at least one hundred days of guaranteed wage employment in a financial year to every household whose adult members volunteer to do unskilled manual work.

The Act came into force on February 2, 2006 and was implemented in a phased manner. In Phase one it was introduced in 200 of the most backward districts of the country. It was implemented in additional 130 districts in Phase two 2007-2008. As per the initial target, MGNREGA was to be expanded countrywide in five years. However, in order to bring the whole nation under its safety net and keeping in view the demand, the Scheme was extended to the remaining 274 rural districts of India from April 1, 2008 in Phase III.

MGNREGA is the first ever law internationally, that guarantees wage employment at an unprecedented scale. The primary objective of the Act is augmenting wage employment. Its auxiliary objective is strengthening natural resource management through works that address causes of chronic poverty like drought, deforestation and soil erosion and so encourages sustainable development. The process outcome includes strengthening grass root processes of democracy and infusing transparency and accountability in governance.

With its rights-based framework and demand driven approach, MGNREGA marks a paradigm shift from the previous wage programmes. The Act is also a significant vehicle for strengthening decentralization and deepening processes of democracy by giving a pivotal role to the Panchayati Raj Institutions in planning, monitoring and implementation. Unique features of the ACT include, time bound employment guarantee and wage payment within 15 days, incentive-disincentive structure to the State Governments for providing employment as 90 percent of the cost for employment provided is borne by the Centre or payment of unemployment allowance at their own cost and emphasis on labour intensive works prohibiting the use of contractors and machinery. The Act also mandates a33 percent participation for women.

Increasing Employment Opportunities: In the first year of implementation 2006-07 in 200 districts, 2.10 crore households were employed and 90.5 crore person days were generated. In 2007-2008, 3.39 crore households were provided employment and 143.5 crore person days generated in 330 districts. In 2008-2009, 4.51 crore households were provided employment and 216.32 crore person days were generated. In 2009-10 (up to December, 2009), 160 crore person days employment has been generated.

Enhancing Wage Earning and Impact on Minimum Wage: The enhanced wage earnings have lead to strengthening of the livelihood resource base of the rural poor in India; in 2007-2008, more than 68 percent of funds utilised were in the form of wages paid to the labourers. In 2008-2009, 73 percent of the funds have been utilized in the form of wages.

Increasing Outreach to the poor: Self targeting in nature, the Programme has high works participation of marginalized groups like SC/ST (57 percent), and women (43 percent) in 2007-2008, In 2008-2009, up to July 2008), the participation of SC/ST was 54 percent and they of women 49 percent.

Strengthening Natural Resource Base of Rural India: In 2007-08, 17.88 lakh works were undertaken, of which 49 percent were related to water conservation. In 2008-2009, (up to July 2008, 27.75 lakh works were undertaken, of which 46 percent are related to water conservation. In 2009-10, 36.51 lakh works were undertaken of which 51 percent constituted water conservation, 16 percent rural connectivity and 14 percent land development.

Financial Inclusion of the poor: The Central government has been encouraging the state governments to make wage payment through bank and post office accounts of wage seekers. In 2009-10, 8.57 lakh bank and post office accounts were opened to disburse wages. The Ministry is also encouraging the MGNREGA workers to obtain insurance under Jan Shri Bima Yojana of LIC.

Initial evidence through independent studies indicates the enhancement of agricultural productivity (through water harvesting, check dams, ground water recharging, improve moisture content, check in soil erosion and micro-irrigation), stemming of distress migration, increased access to markets and services through rural connectivity works, supplementing household incomes, increase in women workforce participation ratios and the regeneration of natural resources.

The vision of the Ministry is enabling MGNREGA become a transformative vehicle of empowering local communities to enhance their livelihood security. The Ministry has taken several steps to ensure that the Scheme is implemented effectively like encouraging decentralized participatory management, improving delivery system and public accountability.

6.3 Integrated Rural Development Programme (IRDP)

The concept of Integrated Rural Development was first mooted in the Central Budget of 1976-77. The Central government took up this programme during 1978-79. The programme was extended to cover the whole country with effect from October 2, 1980 on uniform basis. The IRDP was imbued with new orientation of ameliorating poverty following an Antyodaya approach. The programme also laid emphasis on formulation of block/cluster plan based on systematic identification of poor families and selection of appropriate activities of them.

The programme was primarily related to integrate approach for the socio-economic development of the rural communities. It was designed to eradicate rural poverty and generate more income especially for the poor sections of the rural society. The basic idea behind this programme was that the strategy for the development is so designed as it may help in creating productivity and production better in the agricultural and non-agricultural sectors in the rural areas. Any development programme which aims at improving the lot of the rural poor must create productive assets for them for improving the productivity of land by providing access to input like water, improved seeds and fertilizers etc. To help the rural poor, it would be an essential step particularly for those who own land. The activities based on local resources will also have to be identified and fully exploited. The development of skills and vocational opportunities backed by the required services has assumed specific significance in IRDP.

The main objective of the IRDP was to help small and marginal farmers, agricultural labourers, rural artisans and other rural poor to cross the poverty line and to create substantial opportunities of employment for these people in the rural sector through productive programmes at block level. The main thrust of IRDP was the transfer of productive assets and thereby broadening the resource base of the poorest of the poor families. Under the programme at least 50 percent of the beneficiaries have to be scheduled castes/scheduled tribes and 40 percent of the assisted should be women. Three percent of IRDP benefits have been earmarked for the physically handicapped.

The IRDP aimed at integration of five majors sectors viz:

1. Agriculture including animal husbandry, fishery, forestry and horticulture,
2. Village, cottage and small industries,
3. Tertiary sector which would cover artisans and the requirements of skilled workers in several rural activities,
4. Employment in various resources that were necessary for the achievement of production and distribution in the fields of comprehensive agriculture and rural industries, and
5. Labour mobilisation training in skills and organized mobility to tie up labour with opportunity.

6.3.1 Operational Strategy of IRDP: The main elements of the operational strategy of IRDP are as under:

1. A five year development profile should be drawn up in each district and desegregated into Blocks, based on practical possibilities of development in all sectors. The plan so formulated provides the framework of action for the development schemes of development in each sector;
2. Preparation of a specific agricultural extra strategy for the small and marginal farmers;
3. A special programme of assistance for the households of the rural poor is to be drawn up by identifying those who are below the poverty line. A households rather than individual approach is to be followed with the objective of economic upliftment of the household through a package of activities involving all working members;
4. In the identification of families below the poverty line the Gram Sabha should be involved and identification should be done in a manner, which would ensure that only those belonging to the target groups are included into the programme;
5. Preparation of a blue print for exploiting the available potential in the secondary and tertiary sectors, spelling out linkages for training and marketing for each Block specially for target group identified for assistance;
6. A suitable mechanism is to be developed to secure representation of the poor in the implementing agencies at the district and block levels to facilitate better planning and implementation of the programme;
7. The credit plan for the district/block should be prepared taking into account the total credit needs of the area, and specifically indicating the credit requirements of the target groups;
8. The programme is to be implemented through a single agency in each district called District Rural Development Agency (DRDA) ensuring adequate autonomy to it so that the agency can formulate and implement the programme effectively. The agency must be fully backed by supports from various concerned departments at the district level;

9. Block organisation should be the field level agency for implementation of IRDP; and
10. IRDP has been conceived essentially as an anti-poverty programme. The objective could be achieved by enabling the poorest of the poor families to acquire productive assets, technology and skill as would make their economic activities viable. At the same time an attempt should also be made to provide social services like health, education and housing to them. The household cantered poverty alleviation strategy, will thus, consist of steps not only for the economic emancipation of the family but also for the education of the children, health and welfare for the vulnerable members adoption of small family norms etc; ultimately improving the quality of life of the rural poor. [2]

The IRDP has been implemented in all the blocks of the country. It is a centrally sponsored programme in which the Centre and States share costs equally.

6.4 Training Rural Youth for Self-employment (TRYSEM)

This programme was started on 15th August, 1979 with the objective of equipping rural youth with necessary skills and technological know-how to make them capable to seek self employment in agriculture and allied activities, industries, services and business activities. Only youths belonging to the families of the target groups of small and marginal farmers, agricultural labourers, rural artisans and others below the poverty line are eligible. Normally persons between the ages of 18 and 35 years are covered under the programme.

Component of the IRDP under the TRYSEM scheme at least 50 percent of youth selected for training must be from scheduled caste/scheduled tribe families and minimum 40 percent should be women among the total trainees. Three percent of the benefits have been earmarked for physically handicapped.

Under this scheme, a suitable stipend up to ₹ 300 per

month and a free tool kit worth about ₹ 600 was given to each trainee. After completion of training, each trained rural youth is given subsidy and credit under IRDP for acquisition of assets suited to do jobs and generate income.

In Uttar Pradesh, the scheme was started in 1979-80 in all the Development Blocks to train the rural youth so as to make them capable of self-employment. The government of India had provided financial assistance to the State to the tune of 50 percent for its implementation. After imparting the training, the youths are also to be given employment in local industries, occupations or services so that they become either self-employed or get salaried employment in such industries, occupations and services. Under the scheme, annually 60,000 youths are being given training in such occupations as mechanic, electrical, welding, repair of hand pumps, repair of pump sets, repair of radios, T.V. and bicycle and 'photography etc.'

Against the target of 10.05 lakh youths to be trained during the Sixth Five Year Plan, 9.4 lakh youths were trained which accounts for 93.3 percent of the target. Of the 9.4 lakh youth trained, 4.64 lakh youth (49.4 percent) were self-employed. Members of SCs/STs accounted for 31.5 percent of the persons trained, while women accounted for 34.8 percent of the total number of persons trained.

During the Seventh Five Year Plan, about 10 lakh youths were trained under this programme, of which over 4.6 lakh are self employed and 1.3 lakh were absorbed in wages employment. During this plan about ₹ 129 crore were spent.

In the Eighth Five Year Plan, upgradation of skills and technology needs have been given emphasis for generating employment opportunities in rural areas. For self-employment, it was necessary to give training for wage employment opportunities and the quality of training would improve the skills of the trainee. The target for providing training to 3,060 lakh youths was set up in the Eighth Five Year Plan. An outlay of ₹ 785 lakh was provided in the Plan.

6.5 Development of Women and Children in Rural Areas (DWCRA)

This new scheme was taken up as part of IRDP in 1982. It was launched by the Department of Rural Development in 50 Blocks on a pilot basis with a view to improve the status and living conditions of women by increasing their income and also to provide support services needed to enable them to take up income generating activities. Women and children would be the focus in services like welfare, health, nutrition and education.

Under the scheme women are organized into groups of 10-15. Each group is given one-time grant of up to ₹ 15,000 as revolving fund for infrastructure, new materials, marketing, child care etc.

In implementing the DWCRA programme, the strategy adopted is one of "group approach". The aim is to bring the women together for economic activities suitable to their ability and skill in planning and formulation as well as for inculcating in them a spirit of community approach. The group may be either in the form of formal registered or informal unregistered group. The one-time grant provided to the group is contributed equally the government of India, state government and UNICEF.

At present the programme has been extended to all the districts in the country and the revolving fund has been increased from ₹ 15,000 to ₹ 25,000 in case of stabilized DWCRA groups who wish to diversity.

The Sixth Five Year Plan [3] outlay for the scheme was ₹ 15.60 crore, which was shared equally by the centre and the states. In addition, UNICEF assistance was ₹ 5.40 crore. In all, 3,308 groups covering 52,170 women beneficiaries were organised under the programme in the Sixth Five Year Plan.

At the end of the Seventh Plan, [4] period this programme was in operation in 161 districts. In this Plan, about 28,000 groups were formed against the target of 35,000 with a membership of 4.6 lakh women.

In the Eighth Five Year Plan [5] encouragement was given to the formation of thrift and credit societies for receiving the contribution from the government and rural women were encouraged to form cooperatives or institutions for self-employment purpose. Besides, emphasis was also on child care.

The plan also provided for markets for the sale of their products. During the Plan, one lakh rural women were provided assistance under this programme and about 5,000 new women groups were organised with an outlay of ₹ 525 lakh.

6.6 Jawahar Rozgar Yojana (JRY)

This programme was launched in the last year of the Seventh Five Year Plan with a total allocation of ₹ 2,600 crore to generate 931 million man days of employment. The primary objective of the scheme is to provide employment to the unemployed members of those families that are living in the rural areas below the poverty line. The objective of the programme has also been the generations of additional employment or productive works, which would either benefit to the poor or contribute to the creation of rural infrastructure that will help, improve quality of life in rural areas.

The two employment generating programmes namely: National Rural Employment Programme and Rural Landless Employment Guarantee Programme were merged into a single new rural employment programme viz., Jawahar Rozgar Yojana (JRY) with effect from 18th April, 1989.

In providing employment, preference is given to SCs/STs. Overriding preference is given to freed bonded labourers. Under the scheme, 30 percent employment has been reserved for women. The expenditure of the scheme shared between the Centre and the State is 80:20. Six percent of funds were earmarked for Indira Awaas Yojana (IAY) for the construction of houses for SCs/STs and the freed bonded labourers who are below poverty line.

The following activities were undertaken in the Eighth Five-Year Plan:

1. Preference was given to scheduled castes and scheduled tribes for providing employment opportunities.
2. 30 percent of the employment opportunities under this programme were reserved for women.
3. For 'Million Wells Scheme,' 20 percent of the outlay was provided.
4. An allocation of 2 percent was provided for administration/contingent expenditure.
5. For 'Indira Awaas Yojana,' about 5 percent of the total outlay was provided.
6. The authority for selecting, sanctioning and implementation of the works, according to the needs of the villages was given to the Gram Panchayats.

During the Eighth Five Year Plan an outlay of ₹ 51,000 lakh was provided including ₹ 4,500 lakh for hill areas.

The JRY has been modified from 1993-94 and is now being implemented in the following three streams:

First Stream: It is on the existing pattern with the two sub-schemes, namely Indira Awaas Yojana (IAY) and Million Wells Scheme (MWS). The resources under this stream are allocated to the States/Union Territories in the proportion of the rural poor in the States/UTs to the total rural poor in the country. 10 percent of the total resources of JRY are earmarked for the IAY and 30 percent for MWS. The funds for the IAY and MWS are operated by the District Rural Development Agencies (DRDA)/Zila Panchayats. After providing for the earmarked sectors of IAY and the MWS, at least 80 percent of the remaining funds are distributed among different village panchayats in the district.

Works undertaken in the first stream include:

1. Social forestry works on government and community lands belonging to panchayat etc., road side plantations, plantations along canal banks, on the side of railways line etc.;

2. Soil and water conservation works;
3. Minor irrigation works;
4. Construction/renovation of village tanks for providing irrigation as well as drinking water;
5. Construction of community sanitary latrines ;
6. Construction of houses for SCs/STs and freed bonded labour;
7. Construction of rural roads;
8. Land Development and reclamation of waste lands;
9. Construction of community centres, panchayat ghars, mobile mandies, market yards, dispensaries, anganwadis, balwadis etc.;
10. Construction of school buildings etc.

Second Streams: In this stream an intensified JRY in 120 identified backward districts with additional allocation has been taken.

Third Stream: In this stream, some special and innovative projects have been under taken. These projects aim at prevention of migration of labour, enhancing women's employment, special programmes through voluntary organisations aiming at drought proofing as well as watershed development waste land development resulting in sustained employment.

Although this programme has made some headway in providing employment but the target of providing 90-100 days of employment of every registered person is a distant goal. Other works done under this programme are also not up to the mark.

6.7 Swarnajayanti Gram Swarozgar Yojana (SGSY)

The Swarnjayanti Gram Swarozgar Yojana (SGSY) was launched as an integrated programme for self-employment of the rural poor with effect from April 1, 1999. The objective of the scheme is to bring the assisted poor families above the poverty line by organising them into self-help groups (SHGs) through the process of social mobilisation, their training and capacity building and provision of income generating assets through a mix of bank credit and government subsidy. The scheme emphasizes establishment of activity clusters through selection of key activities based on aptitude and skill of the people, availability of resources and market potentiality. The scheme adopts a process approach and attempts to build the capacities of the rural poor. It provides for involvement of NGOs/CBOs/Individuals/Banks and/self-help promoting institutions in nurturing and development of SHGs, including skill development. The scheme provides for the cost of social intermediation and skill development training based on the local requirements. Flexibility has been given to the DRDAs/ States in the utilisation of funds for training, sanction of Revolving Fund, subsidy for economic activity based on the stage of development of groups.

The focus of the programme is on establishing a large number of micro-enterprises in rural areas based on the ability of the poor and potential of each area, both land-based and otherwise, for sustainable income generation.

Due emphasis is being laid on different components such as capacity building of the poor, skill development training, credit training, technology transfer, marketing and infrastructure.

The subsidy allowed under the SGSY is 30 percent of the total project cost, subject to a ceiling of ₹ 7,500 (for SC/STs and disabled persons subsidy limit is 50 percent of the project cost subject to a ceiling of ₹ 10,000). For self-help groups (SHGs), subsidy would be 50 percent of the project cost subject to a ceiling of ₹ 1.25 lakh or per capita subsidy of ₹ 10,000, whichever is less. There is no monetary ceiling on subsidy for minor irrigation projects for SHGs as well as individual swarozgaris.

The SGSY has a special focus on the vulnerable groups among the rural poor, SC/STs account for at least 50 percent, women 40 percent and the persons with physical disability constitute 3 percent of the Swarozgaris respectively. The

SGSY seeks to promote multiple credits rather than a one-time credit injection.

The SHGs may consist of 10-20 members. In case of minor irrigation workers, disabled persons and desert areas, i.e. hilly, desert and sparsely populated areas, this number may be a minimum of five. Self-help groups should also be drawn from the BPL list approved by the Gram Sabha. The SHGs broadly go through three stages of evolution such as group formation, capital formation through the revolving fund and skill development and taking up of economic activity for income generation.

Selection could be made up to 10 key activities per block based on local resources, occupational skills of the people and availability of market so that the Swarozgaris can draw suitable incomes from their investment. Under SGSY, each block should concentrate on 4-5 selected key activities and attend to all aspects of these activities in a cluster approach, so that swarozgaris can draw sustainable income from their investments. The scheme lays special emphasis on development of swarozgaris through well designed training courses. SGSY is being implemented through the District Rural Development Agencies (DRDAs), with active involvement of panchayati raj institutions, banks and NGOs. It is financed on 75:25 cost-sharing basis between the Centre and the states.

By now 36.78 lakh SHGs have been formed out of which 24.09 lakh SHGs have passed Grade I and 11.24 lakh have passed Grade II, while 8.36 lakh have taken up economic activities. During 2009-10, (till December 2009), 11.65 lakh swarozgaries have been assisted out of which 7.85 lakh are women (67.36 percent).

The percentage of Credit mobilisation has increased over the years from 12.96 percent in 1999-2000 to 89.83 percent in the year 2009-10. The total credit target for the year 2009-10 was ₹ 2504.64 crore (56.36 percent). A close coordination between different agencies responsible for implementation of

SGSY is vital for the success of the programme.

6.8 Sampoorna Grameen Rozgar Yojana (SGRY)

The Sampoorna Grameen Rozgar Yojana (SGRY) was launched on September 25, 2001 by merging the on-going schemes of Employment Assurance Scheme (EAS) and Jawahar Gram Samridh Yojana (JGSY) with the objective of providing additional wage employment and food security, alongside creation of durable community assets in rural areas. The programme is self-targeting in nature with provisions for special emphasis on women, scheduled castes, scheduled tribes and parents of children withdrawn from hazardous occupations.

The annual outlay for the programme is ₹ 10,000 crore which includes 50 lakh tonnes on food grains. Food grains are provided free of cost to the States/UTs. The payment of food grains is made directly to FCI at economic cost by the Centre. However, State Governments are responsible for the cost of transportation of food grains from FCI godown to work-site/PDS shops and its distribution.

The programme is implemented by all the three tiers of Panchayati Raj Institutions. Each level of Panchayat is an independent unit for formulation of Action Plan and executing the scheme. Resources are distributed among District Panchayats, Intermediate Panchayats and the Gram Panchayats in the ratio of 20:30:50.

This programme is executed through two streams, viz:

First Stream: It replaces the EAS, which is implemented at the District and intermediate Panchayat levels. Out of the total fund available under SGRY, 50 percent is earmarked and distributed between the Zila Parishads (20 percent) and the intermediate level Panchayats or Panchayat Samities (30 percent). [6]

Second Stream: It replaces JGSY and is implemented at the Village Panchayat level. 50 percent of the SGRY fund is earmarked for this stream.

The scheme envisages generation of 100 crore man days of wage employment in a year. The programme being a centrally sponsored scheme is implemented on a cost sharing basis between the Centre and the State in the ratio of 75:25.

The Gram Panchayats can take up any work with the approval of the Gram Sabha as per their need and within available funds. 50 percent of the fund earmarked to the Gram Panchayats are utilized for infrastructure development works in SC/ST localities. Five kg. of foodgrains will be made available per man day to the workers and the balance of wages will be paid in cash. For overall supervision of the programme, Zila Parishads have been made responsible.

6.9 Pradhan Mantri Gram Sadak Yojana (PMGSY)

The Pradhan Mantri Gram Sadak Yojna (PMGSY) was launched on 25th December 2000 as a fully funded Centrally Sponsored Scheme. The primary objective of the PMGSY is to provide connectivity to all the eligible unconnected habitations of more than 500 persons in the rural areas (250 persons in the hilly and desert areas) by good quality all-weather roads. 1,36,464 habitations were targeted under the scheme.

Under Bharat Nirman, goal has been set to provide connectivity to all the habitations with population of more than 1000 in the plain areas and habitations with a population of 500 or more in hilly and tribal areas in a time-bound manner by 2009. The systematic upgradation of the existing rural road networks is also an integral component of the scheme. Accordingly, an Action Plan has been prepared for connecting 66,802 habitations with 1,46,185 km. of all-weather roads.

This Action Plan also envisages upgradation/renewal of 1,94,130 km. of the existing rural road network. Subsequently, based on ground verification by States, 62,985 habitations were found eligible to be connected under the programme, out of which 3,421 habitations have been connected under other schemes. Thus, the revised target is to connect 59,564 habitations. It is estimated that an investment of about

₹ 48,000 crore would be required for achieving the targets under Bharat Nirman. The implementation strategy focuses on quality, cost management and 'on time' delivery.

Till December 2009, a total of 33,812 habitations have been connected by constructing 97,583 km. rural roads. In addition, 1,84,353 km. of existing rural roads have been upgraded/renewed. Projects for connecting 20,067 habitations are at different stages implementation.

6.10 Indira Awaas Yojana (IAY)

The Government of India is implementing Indira Awaas Yojana (IAY) since the year1985-86 to provide financial assistance for construction/upgradation of dwelling units to the below poverty line (BPL) rural households belonging to the scheduled castes, scheduled Tribes and freed bonded labourers categories. From the year 1993-94, the scope of the scheme was extended to cover non-scheduled caste and scheduled tribes rural BPL poor, subject to the condition that the benefits to non-SC/ST would not be more than 40 percent of the total IAY allocation. The benefits of the Scheme have also been extended to the families of ex-servicemen of the armed and paramilitary forces killed in action, 3 percent of the Houses are reserved for the rural Below Poverty Line physically and mentally challenged persons. From 2006-07 onwards, funds and physical targets under IAY are also being earmarked for BPL minorities in each state.

Under the scheme, financial resources are shared between the centre and the states on a 75:25 basis. Since, reduction of shelter lessens is the primary objective,75 percent weightage is given to housing shortage and 25 percent to the poverty ratios prescribed by Planning Commission for state level allocation. For district level allocation, 75 percent weightage is given again to housing shortage and 25 percent to SC/ST population of the concerned districts.

On the basis of allocations made and targets fixed, district Rural development Agency (DRDAs)/Zilla Parishada (ZPs) decide Panchayat-wise number of houses to be constructed under IAY and intimate the same to the concerned Gram Panchayat. Thereafter, the Gram Sabha selects the beneficiaries, restricting its number to the target allotted, from the list of eligible households from the Permanent IAY Wait lists. No further approval of the higher authority is required.

The ceiling on construction assistance under the IAY has been enhanced w.e.f. 1.4.2008: ₹ 25, 000 to ₹ 35,000 per unit in the plain areas and from ₹ 27,500 to ₹ 38,500 in hilly/difficult areas. For upgradation of kutcha house, the financial assistance has also been enhanced from ₹ 12,500 to ₹ 15,000 per unit. In addition, the Reserve Bank of India has been requested by the Ministry of Finance to include IAY houses under the Differential Rate of Interest (DRI) scheme for lending up to ₹ 20,000 per unit at an interest rate of 4 percent.

Further, the dwelling units should invariably be allotted in the name of a female member of the beneficiary household. Alternatively, it can be allotted in the name of both husband and wife. Only in case there is no eligible female member in the family, the house can be allotted in the name of an eligible male member.

The Sanitary latrine and smokeless chullah and proper drainage are required for each IAY house. Latrine could be constructed separate for the IAY house on the site of beneficiary.

The construction of the houses is the sole responsibility of the beneficiary. Engagement of contractors is strictly prohibited.

No specific type design has been stipulated for an IAY house. Choice of design, technology and materials for construction of an IAY house is the sole discretion of the beneficiaries.

About 218.69 lakh houses have been constructed under IAY since inception of the Scheme with an expenditure of ₹ 52,366 crore (up to 11.1.2010).

6.11 Nehru Rozgar Yojana (NRY)

This scheme was launched in 1989. It caters to the economic needs of the Urban poor, mainly the unemployed and under employed by providing them employment opportunities through skill up-gradation assistance in setting up their own micro-enterprises and scheme for shelter and housing upgradation. The NRY further has three sub-themes:

1. The Scheme of Urban Micro Enterprises (SUME).
2. The Scheme of Urban Wage Employment (SUWE).
3. The Scheme of Housing and Shelters Up-gradation (SHASU).

6.12 Swarna Jayanti Shahri Rozgar Yojana (SJSR)

This scheme was approved in 1997. There are two sub-schemes under this scheme, namely,

1. Urban Self-employment Programme (USEP).
2. Urban Wage Employment Programme (UWEP).

The USEP shall apply to all urban areas irrespective of the size of the population and UWEP to apply to centres with population less than 5 lakh as per 1991 census.

This scheme is funded on a 75:25 basis between the Centre and the States.

6.13 Watershed Development Programmes

The Department of Land Resources in the Ministry of Rural Development is administering three area-based watershed programmes for development of wastelands/ degraded lands namely Drought Prone Areas Programmes (DPAP), Desert Development Programme (DDP) and Integrated Wastelands Development Programme (IWDP) to check the diminishing productivity of wasteland and loss of natural resources.

The DPAP was launched in 1973-74 to tackle the special problems faced by those areas that are constantly afflicted by drought conditions. Presently, 972 blocks of 195 districts in 16 States are covered under the Programme. DDP was launched in 1977-78 to mitigate the adverse effects of decertification. Presently, 235 blocks of 40 districts in 7 States are covered under the Programme. IWDP has been under implementation since 1989-90. The projects under the IWDP are generally sanctioned in areas that are not covered under DDP or DPAP.

Since 1 April 1995, these three programmes are being implemented on the basis of Common Guidelines for Watershed Development. Details of projects sanctioned and funds released from 1995-96 to 2007-2008 are given in Table 6.1.

Table 6.1: Projects Sanctioned and Funds Released

Name of Scheme	No. of project Sanctioned	Area Covered (in lakh)	Total Funds released (₹ crore)
DPAP	27,439	130.20	2,837.81
DDP	15,746	78.73	2,103.23
IWDP	1,877	107.0	2,797.56
Grand total	45,062	322.93	7,738.60

The projects under DPAP and DDP are sanctioned for 500 ha. each while the IWDP projects cover an area of 5000-6000 ha.

The cost norms for all the three schemes have been revised to ₹ 6000 per ha. under DPAP and DDP, it is shared between the Centre and the States in ratio of 75:25. In case of IWDP, the cost sharing between the Centre and State Governments is in the ratio of 11:1.

Funds are released in seven instalments, six instalments at the rate of 15 percent and the last instalment at the rate of 10 percent. The first instalment is released along with the initial sanction-order and subsequent instalments on receipt of utilization for 50 percent of the available funds as well as the following documents: (a) Quarterly Progress Reports; (b) Utilisation Certificates; (c) The Audited Statement of Accounts for the previous years; and (d) Evidence of satisfactory completion of institutional arrangements.

Projects are implemented by District Rural Development Agencies/Zilla Parishads (DRDAs/ZPs) through Project Implementing Agencies (PIAs). PIAs could be a Line Department (of the State Government), Panchayati Raj Institutions or reputed NGOs. One PIA normally handles 10-12 watershed projects covering an area of about 5,000-6,000 hectares. The PIA is required to maintain a technical team of 4 experts called Watershed Development Team (WDT) and individual projects (500hectares) are planned and executed by the local people living in the watershed area called the Watershed Association (WA) through an elected body called Watershed Committee (WC).

The Department of Land Resources has brought out a new initiative called 'Hariyali' with an objective of empowering PRIs both financially and administratively in implementation of Watershed Development Programmes. Under this initiative, all ongoing area development programmes namely, Integrated Wastelands Development Programme (IWDP), Drought Prone Areas Programme (DPAP) and Desert Development Programme (DDP) are to be implemented through the PRIs. New projects under the aforesaid area development programmes are being implemented in accordance with the guidelines for Hariyali from 1 April 2003.

Projects sanctioned prior to this date shall continue to be implemented as per the Watershed Development Guidelines of 2001.

In the new arrangement, Gram Panchayats shall implement projects under over all supervision and guidance of Project Implementation Agencies (PIAs). An intermediate panchayat may be the PIA for all the projects sanctioned to a particular Block/Taluka. In case, these Panchayats are not adequately empowered, then the Zilla Panchayat can either act as PIA itself or may appoint a suitable Line Department like Agriculture, Forestry/Social Forestry, Soil Conservation, etc., or an Agency of the State Government/University/Institute as

PIA. Failing these options, the ZP/DRDA may consider appointing a reputed Non-Government Organization (NGO) in the district with adequate experience and expertise in the implementation of watershed projects or related area development works as the PIA after thoroughly examining their credentials.

The Project Implementing Agency (PIA) will provide necessary technical guidance to the Gram Panchayat for preparation of development plans for the watershed through Participatory Rural Appraisal (PRA) exercise, under take community organisation and training for the village communities, supervise watershed development activities, inspect and authenticate project accounts.

6.14 Special Employment Scheme by Khadi and Gramodyog Board

In Uttar Pradesh Khadi and Gramodyog Board is implementing the schemes of training in New Model Charkha and self-employment. Such schemes are being implemented for the women of Scheduled Castes, Scheduled Tribes, minorities and weaker sections (living in rural areas of the State). The objective of all these schemes is to arrange work for these women at their houses and effect qualitative improvement in their economic and social conditions.

6.15 Antyodaya Anna Yojana (AAY)

The scheme was launched in December 2000. Under the scheme 1 crore poorest families out of the BPL families covered under the Targeted Public Distribution System are identified. 35 kg. of food grains are made available to each eligible family at a highly subsidized rate of ₹ 2 per kg. for wheat and ₹ 3 per kg. for rice.

6.16 Ambedkar Vishesh Rozgar Yojana (AVRY)

This scheme is being implemented by the government of Uttar Pradesh. The main objectives of this scheme are as follows:

1. To implement plans for generating employment;
2. To create opportunities for continuous employment;
3. To increase the incomes of rural families; and
4. To create an effective marketing system for selling/distributing product manufactured in rural areas by keeping in view the available local resources and requirements of rural areas.

In the beginning of this scheme, sixty seven different projects were approved in various districts of the State. It has been done keeping in view the local requirements and demands of the people of those districts.

The above mentioned programmes and schemes are directly related to making the gainful employment opportunities available to rural and urban women in various occupations and to improving their economic and social status. There are also several programmes and schemes, which are indirectly related to improving the lot of women worker, who are engaged in informal sector in the state such as Ambedkar Rural Urban Small Enterprises Scheme, Urban Labour Scheme etc.

6.17 Social Security Act, 2008

In December 2008, The Unorganized Sector Worker's Social Security Act was passed by both houses of Parliament amidst controversy. The Act goes no further than accepting in principle that social security should be provided to unorganized sector workers. No new schemes were announced and no specific financial allocation made (The Rashtriya Swasthaya Bima Yojna predates the passage of this Act and is restricted only to BPL families). Even the Rules of this Act have not been notified. The Act is no more than a statement of intent, which leaves the task of formulating social security schemes to State Governments and subsequent Union Governments. The Act mandates respective State Governments to constitute State Level Boards for formulating social security and welfare schemes, but these boards only have advisory powers.

Despite several shortcomings, the Act states that social security is a right of all unorganized sector workers. With growing casualization and informalization of work in the country it is about time that the Union and state governments take concrete steps in this regard. The governments of West Bengal and Tripura started a contributory provident fund scheme in the years 2000 and 2002, respectively, for all unorganized sector workers of their states. If a worker saves ₹ 1 a day then the government also adds the same amount to their account with EPF interest rates. In our three years old campaign among home-based women workers of Delhi, we find that women spontaneously favour the formulation of such a scheme in Delhi from among the various examples of social security schemes from across the country. Their choice is based on an assessment of what they can manage to save in a day.

The Janwadi Mahila Samiti demands the following from the Delhi government:

1. Recognize home-based women workers. Provide immediate registration and I-cards/'Smart Cards' to all home-based workers.
2. Constitute a State Level Board for formulating social security and welfare schemes for all home-based workers.
3. Provide social security cover, i.e., pension, health insurance, maternity benefits, provident fund, housing and education cover to all home-based workers.
4. Provide BPL ration cards to all home-based workers.
5. Provide skill upgradation and other assistance to all home-based workers.

It is about time that the government wakes up to the stark reality of lakh of home-based women workers in Delhi and takes concrete steps in recognition of their work, condition and contribution.

6.18 Social Security Scheme

In India, the term social security is generally used in its broadest sense, it may consist of all types of measures preventive, promotional and protective as the case may be. The measures may be statutory, public or private. The term encompasses social insurance, social assistance, social protection, social safety net and other steps involved.

There are number of schemes which provide social security to the workers in the unorganised sector. These may be classified as under:

1. Centrally funded social assistance programmes.
2. Social insurance scheme.
3. Social assistance through welfare funds of Central and State Governments.
4. Public initiatives.

Centrally funded social assistance programmes: include the employment oriented poverty alleviation programmes such as Swarnjayanti Gram Swarojgar Yojana, Jawahar Gram Samridhi Yojana, and Employment Assurance Scheme. National Social Assistance Programme (NSAP) comprising old age pension, family benefit and maternity benefits to address the social security needs of the people below poverty line.

The social insurance schemes include several schemes launched by the Central and the State Governments for the benefit of weaker sections through the Life Insurance Corporation of India and General Insurance Corporation of India. There are schemes for the employees of shops and commercial establishment and other weaker sections. 'Janshree Bima Yojana' is a group insurance scheme and covers natural/accidental death, partial or total permanent disability due to accident and the people below poverty line and marginally above are eligible to join the Scheme. Another group insurance scheme for the agriculture landless labour, 'Krishi Shramik Samajik Suraksha Yojana, 2001' launched in July, 2001 provides for pension and insurance besides providing money back. The contribution of the beneficiary is ₹ 1 per day while the Government contributes ₹ 2 per day Several public institutions and agencies are also imparting various kinds of social security benefits to the selected groups of workers. Among these Self-Employed Women's Association (SEWA) has made significant achievement in promoting social security through the formation of cooperatives.

Welfare funds represent one of the models developed in India for providing social protection to workers in the unorganised sector. The Government of India has set up five welfare funds. Central funds are administered through the Ministry of Labour for the beedi and workers in certain other occupations for whom no direct employers-employee relationship exists and is implemented without any contribution from the Government. The scheme of welfare fund is outside the framework of specific employer and employee relationship in as much as the resources are raised by the Government on non-contributory basis and the delivery of welfare services is effected without linkage to individual worker's contribution. These funds are constituted from the cess collected from the employers and manufacturers/producers of particular commodity/industry concerned.

The Government has also enacted a Central legislation for the building and other construction workers towards creation of welfare funds at the level of States. There are around 20 million construction workers in the country. A small cess is collected on the basis of the cost of a construction project which makes the corpus of the welfare fund for the construction workers. All facilities as enumerated above are provided to this section of the unorganised sector workers. Presently three States in the country namely, Kerala, Tamil Nadu and Delhi have started implementing schemes under this Act. However, other States are in the process of adopting.

Moreover, the welfare fund models have successfully been

implemented by various States for various categories of workers. The State of Tamil Nadu is running 11 Welfare Boards for workers like construction workers, truck drivers, footwear workers, handloom and silk weaving workers. Similarly, State of Kerala are also running several welfare funds for agricultural workers, cashew workers, coir workers, fisherman, toddy-tappers etc. The model is so popular that some of the other States like Andhra Pradesh, Karnataka and Madhya Pradesh are in the process of bringing out their own legislation for creation of welfare funds in the unorganised sector workers for providing them social security.

With a budgetary outlay of over ₹ 70,000 crore on various poverty alleviation and employment generation schemes, nearly four and half crore households have availed job opportunities.

"During the year 2009-10, 4.34 crore households have been provided employment under the National Rural Employment Guarantee Scheme (NREGS)," according to Economic Survey, 2009-10.

In the previous financial year, over 4.51 crore households were provided employment under the scheme. As against the budgetary outlay of ₹ 39,100 crore for 2009-10 for NREGS, an amount of ₹ 24,758.50 crore has been released to the States and union territories till December 2009, the Survey, tabled in Parliament, said.

"Out of the 182.88 crore person days created under the scheme during this period, 29 percent and 22 percent were in favour of Schedule Castes and Schedule Tribes population respectively, and 50 percent in favour of women," it added. Under the Swarnjayanti Gram Swarozgar Yojana (SGSY), over 36.78 lakh self-help groups had been formed and 1.33 crore 'swarozgaries' have been assisted with a total investment of ₹ 30,896.08 crore.

The Government has also utilised ₹ 363.12 crore till December 2009 under the Swarna Jayanti Shahari Rozgar Yojana. A total of 28,613 urban poor have been assisted to set up individual enterprises.

Out of the 182.88 crore person days created under the scheme during (2010) this period, 29 percent and 22 percent were in favour of schedule castes and schedule tribes population respectively, and 50 percent in favour of women, the survey said.

6.19 Report of the National Commission on Labour

The achievement of independence contributed in quickening the process of westernization. The Science and technology played a very significant role in this process. The development of industrialisation and communication changed the whole order of the society. These changes have not left the women untouched. The traditional position of the Indian women underwent a change. The women started to play a direct economic role as wage earners in farms, construction sites, factories etc. but they were employed as cheap substitute manual labour. Gradually, the proportion of women in the informal sector has increased but there is a discrimination against women in employment. The following factors are mainly responsible for this discrimination.

1. There is a notion that a man should earn enough to feed his wife and children while women should stay at home and do the house work, childcare etc. This concept has been accepted even by trade unions.
2. 'The women are solely responsible for running the home', this assumption has been a strong support for the introduction of protective legislation. It has been stated that introduction of protective legislation is an important reason for managements' preference for male workers. Thus, they discriminate against women in recruitment.
3. The idea 'industry as the main domain of men' is also an important reason for discrimination against women. In industrial employment as well as in other wage work, there is the segregation of men and women into different types of jobs. In industries, women are mostly employed in jobs

like assembling, packing etc., while engineering electrical and mechanical jobs are given to men. This division concludes in the division into low-paid and high paid jobs. As a matter of fact jobs, which require higher degree of education, skill and training, are better paid. As the women have less access to education and training, they are mostly excluded from better paid jobs. Thus, in industries as well as in works requiring high skill and training, women are concentrated in the more labour intensive and low-paid jobs.

4. The automation is also a very prominent reason for discrimination against women. It has decreased the number of women workers in the organised sector. For example, in many industries like textiles, pharmaceuticals etc., jobs where women were employed such as cotton cleaning, reeling and winding in cotton textiles, packing and assembly in pharmaceutical etc., have drastically reduced due to automation of the production process.

   The women are said to be unfit for heavy manual work and thus, discriminated against in certain jobs. The legislations prohibit the employment of women on load transport during pregnancy and for ten weeks following confinement. However, in their household duties and in the informal head-loads are assigned the heaviest of work such as carrying head-loads of water for long distance, carrying heavy head-loads in construction, mining works etc; manual grinding of corns etc. when there heavy works are replaced by machines, the women are termed as unskilled and are discriminated again.

5. In the organized sector employers assessment of women workers is that they are most expensive and the least flexible labour force. The women's' work at the factory or any other work site constitutes only half of their total work as they perform their household duties also. As this is not true in case of men, they are often more prepared to work overtime for long hours. Thus, the men are more flexible

as they have almost no responsibility at home. The women, therefore, resist to compulsory overtime or increasing workloads.

In the informal sector, however, the situation is almost different. In this sector, unions are absent and legal rights of workforce are much weaker. As the women workers are supposed to be only secondary wage-earner in this sector, they can afford to work for lesser wages. Moreover, as women workers have no other choice they are forced to continue in informal sector despite very low wages and unsatisfactory working conditions. From the employers' point of view, women in the organized sector are most expensive and least-flexible, while in the informal sector they are least expensive and most flexible.

The factors responsible for discrimination against women in employment and their other compulsions have forced the women workers to concentrate in the informal sector.

As there are no organization of women workers in the informal sectors, it has several implications viz:

1. Women workers in this sector work and live in appalling conditions.
2. As this sector is scattered and wider spread-it is difficult to organise the workers.
3. In this sector employers have more bargaining power and control than the workforce.

In this informal sector, where 94 percent of women workers are employed, their status is completely unprotected, as they have no self organisations. This position exists in Bulandshahr district also. During the survey, it was brought to my notice that they had attempted again and again to organize and to struggle but their attempts were brutally crushed. They could only say that their only means of survival had been snatched from them.

End Notes

1. Publication Division, Ministry of Information and Broadcasting, Government of India, "India-2004", p. 505.

2. Tripathi, R.N., "IRDP in South India-An Evaluation", National Institute of Rural Development, Hyderabad, 1985, pp. 2-3.
3. Government of India, Sixth Five Year Plan (1980-85), Planning Commission, New Delhi.
4. Government of India, Seventh Five Year Plan (1985-90), Planning Commission, New Delhi.
5. Government of India, Eighth Five Year Plan (1992-97), Planning Commission, New Delhi.
6. Publication Division, Ministry of Information and Broadcasting, Government of India, "India-2004", p. 585.

7

National Policy for Empowerment of Women (NPEW), 2001

Policies and programmes for welfare, development and empowerment of women in India have been built upon strong commitments by the government and unflagging effort by the women's movement. India's commitment to gender equality is further evidenced by the fact that it is a signatory to Convention on the Elimination of All Forms of Discrimination against Women (CEDAW), which was ratified on June 25, 1993 (with one reservation and two declaratory statements). India is also a signatory to the Convention on the Rights of the Child. The first report to the UN Committee of Experts on the Rights of the Child was submitted in 2000 and the second report in 2004.

In pursuance of the avowed objective of empowering the *women* as agents of socio-economic change, the National Policy on Empowerment of Women was adopted in April 2001. Gender inequality arising out of social norms and cultural traditions has been addressed through a range of direct and indirect measures, and the aim of the NPEW has been to bring about social change—changes in attitudes towards women, and women's empowerment. The policy itself reflects the aspirations of women and the women's movement. The effort is to bring gender justice and make *de jure* equality into *de facto* equality. Several State Governments have also formulated a policy for women's empowerment.

On the basis of NPEW, the National Plan of Action is being implemented which includes the following strategies:

1. To create an enabling environment for women to exercise their rights both within and outside their homes.
2. To reserve one-third of seats for women in the Lok Sabha

and State Legislative Assemblies.

3. To adopt a special strategy for Women Component Plan to ensure that at least 30 percent of funds and benefits flow to women from all development sectors.
4. To organize women in self-help groups as a mark of the beginning of empowering them.
5. To accord high priority and ensure easy access to maternal and child health services.
6. To initiate steps for eliminating gender bias in all educational programmes; further to institute plans for free education of girls up to college levels including professional levels.
7. To equip women with necessary skills in modern upcoming trades which would make them economically independent and self-reliant.
8. To increase women's access to credit through setting up of Development Bank for women entrepreneurs in small and tiny sectors.

Various aspects of NPEW are as under.

7.1 Introduction

The principle of gender equality is enshrined in the Indian Constitution in its Preamble, Fundamental Rights, Fundamental Duties and Directive Principles of State Policy. The Constitution not only grants equality to women, but also empowers the State to adopt measures of positive discrimination in favour of women. Since Independence in 1947, there has been a marked shift in the approach to issues related to welfare, development and empowerment of women. Within the framework of a democratic polity, India's laws, development policies, schemes/programmes under Five Year Plans have aimed at advancement of women in different spheres. In recent years, the empowerment of women has been recognized as the central issue in determining the status of women. The National Commission for Women was set up by an Act of Parliament in 1990 to safeguard the rights and legal entitlements of women. The 73rd and 74th Amendments to the Constitution of India provided for reservation of seats for women in panchayats and municipalities, laying a strong foundation for their participation in decision-making at the local levels.

India has also ratified various international conventions and human rights instruments committing to secure equal rights for women. Key among them is the ratification of the Convention on Elimination of All Forms of Discrimination against Women (CEDAW) in 1993.

The Mexico Plan of Action (1975), the Nairobi Forward Looking Strategies (1985), the Beijing Declaration as well as the Platform for Action (1995) and the Outcome Document—adopted by the General Assembly Session of the United Nations on Gender Equality and Development and Peace for the 21st Century—titled "Further Actions and Initiatives to Implement the Beijing Declaration and the Platform for Action" have been unreservedly endorsed by India for appropriate follow up.

7.2 Objectives of the Policy

National Policy for Empowerment of Women, 2001 was formulated for bringing about advancement, development and empowerment of women in all spheres of life through creation of a more responsive judicial and legal system sensitive to women and mainstreaming a gender perspective in the development process. The strengthening and formation of relevant institutional mechanisms and implementation of international obligations/commitments and co-operation at the international, regional and sub-regional level was another commitment.

The primary objective of NPEW was to bring about the advancement, development and empowerment of women. Specifically, the objectives of this Policy included the following:

1. Creating an environment through positive economic and

social policies for full development of women to enable them to realize their full potential.

2. The *de-jure* and *de-facto* enjoyment of all human rights and fundamental freedom by women on equal basis with men in all spheres—political, economic, social, cultural and civil.
3. Equal access to participation and decision-making of women in social, political and economic life of the nation.
4. Equal access to women to healthcare, quality education at all levels, career and vocational guidance, employment, equal remuneration, occupational health and safety, social security and public office etc.
5. Strengthening legal systems aimed at elimination of all forms of discrimination against women.
6. Changing societal attitudes and community practices by active participation and involvement of both men and women.
7. Mainstreaming a gender perspective in the development process.
8. Elimination of discrimination and all forms of violence against women and the girl child.
9. Building and strengthening partnerships with civil society, particularly women's organizations.

7.3 Various Elements of NPEW

7.3.1 Politico-legal Empowerment of Women

A. Legal-Judicial System: Legal-judicial system would be made more responsive and gender sensitive to women's needs, especially in cases of domestic violence and personal assault. New laws would be enacted and existing laws reviewed to ensure that justice is quick and the punishment meted out to the culprits is commensurate with the severity of the offence.

At the initiative of and with the full participation of all stakeholders including community and religious leaders, NPEW would aim to encourage changes in personal laws such as those related to marriage, divorce, maintenance and guardianship so as to eliminate discrimination against women.

The evolution of property rights in a patriarchal system has contributed to the subordinate status of women. NPEW would aim to encourage changes in laws relating to ownership of property and inheritance by evolving consensus in order to make them gender just.

B. Decision-making: Women's equality in power sharing and active participation in decision making, including decision-making in political process at all levels would be ensured for the achievement of the goals of empowerment. All measures would be taken to guarantee women equal access to and full participation in decision-making bodies at every level, including the legislative, executive, judicial, corporate, statutory bodies, as also the advisory commissions, committees, boards, trusts etc. Affirmative action such as reservations/quotas, including in higher legislative bodies, will be considered whenever necessary on a time-bound basis. Women–friendly personnel policies will also be drawn up to encourage women to participate effectively in the developmental process.

C. Mainstreaming a Gender Perspective in the Development Process: Policies, programmes and systems would be established to ensure mainstreaming of women's perspectives in all developmental processes, as catalysts, participants and recipients. Wherever there are gaps in policies and programmes, women-specific interventions would be undertaken to bridge these. Coordinating and monitoring mechanisms will also be devised to assess, from time to time, the progress of such mainstreaming mechanisms. Issues and concerns related to women would be specifically addressed and reflected in all concerned laws, sectoral policies, plans and programmes of action.

7.3.2 Economic Empowerment of Women:

A. Poverty Eradication: Since women comprise the majority of the population below the poverty line and are very often in situations of extreme poverty—given the harsh realities of intra-household and social discrimination, —macro economic policies and poverty eradication programmes would specifically address the needs and problems of such women. There would be improved implementation of programmes which are already women-oriented with special targets for women. Steps would be taken for mobilization of poor women and convergence of services, by offering them a range of economic and social options, along with necessary support measures to enhance their capabilities.

B. Micro Credit: In order to enhance women's access to credit for consumption and production, establishment of new and strengthening of existing micro-credit mechanisms and micro-finance institution would be undertaken so that the outreach of credit is enhanced. Other supportive measures would be taken to ensure adequate flow of credit through extant financial institutions and banks so that all women below poverty line have easy access to credit.

C. Women and Economy: Women's perspectives would be included in designing and implementing macroeconomic and social policies by institutionalizing their participation in such processes. Their contribution to socio-economic development as producers and workers would be recognized in the formal and informal sectors (including home-based workers) and appropriate policies relating to employment and to her working conditions would be drawn up. Such measures could include the following:

1. Reinterpretation and redefinition of conventional concepts of work wherever necessary (e.g. in the census records), to reflect contribution of women as producers and workers.
2. Preparation of satellite and national accounts.
3. Development of appropriate methodologies for undertaking (1) and (2) above.

D. Globalization: Globalization—the gender impact of which has not been evaluated fully—has presented new challenges for the realization of the goal of women's equality.

It is evident that there is a need for re-framing policies for access to employment and quality of employment.

Benefits of the growing global economy have been unevenly distributed leading to wider economic disparities, the feminization of poverty, increased gender inequality through deteriorating working conditions and unsafe working environment especially in the informal economy and rural areas. Strategies would be designed to enhance the capacity of women and empower them to meet the negative social and economic impacts, which may flow from the globalization process.

E. Women and Agriculture: In view of the critical role of women in the agriculture and allied sectors as producers, concentrated efforts would be made to ensure that benefits of various programmes/schemes reach them in proportion to their numbers. The programmes for training women in soil conservation, social forestry, dairy development and other occupations allied to agriculture (like horticulture, livestock including small animal husbandry, poultry, fisheries etc.) would be expanded to benefit women workers in the agriculture sector.

F. Women and Industry: The important role played by women in electronics, information technology, food processing, agro industry and textiles has been crucial for the development of these sectors. They would be given comprehensive support in terms of labour legislation, social security and other support services to participate in various industrial sectors.

Women at present cannot work in night shift in factories even if they wish to. Suitable measures will be taken to enable women to work on the night shift in factories. This would be accompanied with support services for security, transportation etc.

G. Support Services: The provision of support services for women—like child care facilities, including crèches at work places and educational institutions, homes for the aged and the disabled—would be expanded and improved to create an enabling environment and to ensure their full cooperation in social, political and economic life. Women-friendly personnel policies would also be drawn up to encourage women to participate effectively in the developmental process.

7.3.3 Social Empowerment of Women:

A. Education: Equal access to education for women and girls would be ensured. Special measures would be taken to eliminate discrimination, universalize education, eradicate illiteracy, create a gender-sensitive educational system, increase enrolment and retention rates of girls and improve the quality of education to facilitate life-long learning as well as development of occupation/vocation/technical skills by women. Reducing the gender gap in secondary and higher education would be a focus area. Sectoral time targets in existing policies would be achieved, with a special focus on girls and women, particularly those belonging to weaker sections including the Scheduled Castes/Scheduled Tribes/Other Backward Classes/Minorities. Gender sensitive curricula would be developed at all levels of educational system in order to address sex stereotyping as one of the causes of gender discrimination.

B. Health: A holistic approach to women's health which includes both nutrition and health services would be adopted and special attention would be given to the needs of women and the girls at all stages of the life cycle. The reduction of infant mortality and maternal mortality, which are sensitive indicators of human development, is a priority concern. NPEW reiterated the national demographic goals for Infant Mortality Rate (IMR), Maternal Mortality Rate (MMR) set out in the National Population Policy, 2000. Women should have access to comprehensive, affordable and quality health care. Measures would be adopted that take into account the reproductive rights of women to enable them to exercise informed choices, their vulnerability to sexual and health problems together with endemic, infectious and communicable diseases such as malaria, TB, and water-borne diseases as well as hypertension and cardio-pulmonary diseases. The social, developmental and health consequences of HIV/AIDS and other sexually transmitted diseases would be tackled from a gender perspective.

To effectively meet problems of infant and maternal mortality, and early marriage, the availability of good and accurate data at micro level on deaths, birth and marriages is required. Strict implementation of registration of births and deaths would be ensured and registration of marriages would be made compulsory.

In accordance with the commitment of the National Population Policy, 2000 to population stabilization, NPEW recognized the critical need of men and women to have access to safe, effective and affordable methods of family planning of their choice and the need to suitably address the issues of early marriages and spacing of children. Interventions such as spread of education, compulsory registration of marriage should impact on delaying the age of marriage so that by 2010 child marriages are eliminated.

Women's traditional knowledge about health care and nutrition would be recognized through proper documentation and its use would be encouraged. The use of Indian and alternative systems of medicine would be enhanced within the framework of overall health infrastructure available for women.

C. Nutrition: In view of the high risk of malnutrition and disease that women face at all the three critical stages, viz. infancy and childhood, adolescent and reproductive phase, focussed attention would be paid to meeting the nutritional needs of women at all stages of the life cycle. This is also important in view of the critical link between the health of adolescent girls, pregnant and lactating women with the health of infant and young children. Special efforts would be made to tackle the problem of macro and micro nutrient deficiencies especially amongst pregnant and lactating women as it leads to various diseases and disabilities.

Intra-household discrimination in nutritional matters vis-à-vis girls and women would be sought to be ended through appropriate strategies. Widespread use of nutrition education would be made to address the issues of intra-household imbalances in nutrition and the special needs of pregnant and lactating women. Women's participation would also be ensured in the planning, superintendence and delivery of the system.

D. Drinking Water and Sanitation: Special attention would be given to the needs of women in the provision of safe drinking water, sewage disposal, toilet facilities and sanitation within accessible reach of households, especially in rural areas and urban slums. Women's participation would be ensured in the planning, delivery and maintenance of such services.

E. Housing and Shelter: Women's perspectives would be included in housing policies, planning of housing colonies and provision of shelter both in rural and urban areas. Special attention would be given for providing adequate and safe housing and accommodation for women including single women, heads of households, working women, students, apprentices and trainees.

F. Environment: Women would be involved and their perspectives reflected in the policies and programmes for environment, conservation and restoration. Considering the impact of environmental factors on their livelihoods, women's participation would be ensured in the conservation of the environment and control of environmental degradation. The vast majority of rural women still depend on the locally available non-commercial sources of energy such as animal dung, crop waste and fuel wood. In order to ensure the efficient use of these energy resources in an environmental friendly manner, NPEW would aim at promoting the programmes of non-conventional energy resources. Women would be involved in spreading the use of solar energy, biogas, smokeless chulahs and other rural application so as to have a visible impact of these measures in influencing eco system and in changing the life styles of rural women.

G. Science and Technology: Programmes would be strengthened to bring about a greater involvement of women in science and technology. These would include measures to motivate girls to take up science and technology for higher education and also ensure that development projects with scientific and technical inputs involve women fully. Efforts to develop a scientific temper and awareness would also be stepped up. Special measures would be taken for their training in areas where they have special skills like communication and information technology. Efforts to develop appropriate technologies suited to women's needs as well as to reduce their drudgery would be given a special focus too.

H. Women in Difficult Circumstances: In recognition of the diversity of women's situations and in acknowledgement of the needs of disadvantaged groups, measures and programmes would be undertaken to provide them with special assistance. These groups include women in extreme poverty, destitute women, women in conflict situations, women affected by natural calamities, women in less developed regions, the disabled widows, elderly women, single women in difficult circumstances, women heading households, those displaced from employment, migrants, women who are victims of marital violence, deserted women and prostitutes etc.

I. Violence against Women: All forms of violence against women, physical and mental, whether at domestic or societal levels, including those arising from customs, traditions or accepted practices shall be dealt with effectively with a view to eliminate its incidence. Institutions and mechanisms for assistance would be created and strengthened for prevention of such violence—including sexual harassment at work place—and for the rehabilitation of the victims of violence and for taking effective action against the perpetrators of such violence. A special emphasis would also be laid on programmes and measures to deal with trafficking in women and girls.

J. Rights of the Girl Child: All forms of discrimination against the girl child and violation of her rights shall be eliminated by undertaking strong measures both preventive and punitive within and outside the family. These would relate specifically to strict enforcement of laws against prenatal sex selection and the practices of female foeticide, female infanticide, child marriage, child abuse and child prostitution etc. Removal of discrimination in the treatment of the girl child within the family and outside and projection of a positive image of the girl child would be actively fostered. There would be special emphasis on the needs of the girl child and earmarking of substantial investments in the areas relating to food and nutrition, health and education, and in vocational education. In implementing programmes for eliminating child labour, there would be a special focus on girl children.

K. Mass Media: Media would be used to portray images consistent with human dignity of girls and women. NPEW would specifically strive to remove demeaning, degrading and negative conventional stereotypical images of women and violence against women. Private sector partners and media networks would be involved at all levels to ensure equal access for women, particularly in the area of information and communication technologies. The media would be encouraged to develop codes of conduct, professional guidelines and other self-regulatory mechanisms to remove gender stereotypes and promote balanced portrayals of women and men.

7.4 Operational Strategies of NPEW

7.4.1 Action Plans: All Central and State Ministries would draw up time bound Action Plans for translating NPEW into a set of concrete actions, through a participatory process of consultation with Central/State Departments of Women and Child Development and National/State Commissions for Women. The Plans would specifically include the following:

1. Measurable goals to be achieved by 2010.

2. Identification and commitment of resources.
3. Responsibilities for implementation of action points.
4. Structures and mechanisms to ensure efficient monitoring, review and gender impact assessment of action points and policies.
5. Introduction of a gender perspective in the budgeting process.

In order to support better planning and programme formulation and adequate allocation of resources, Gender Development Indices (GDI) would be developed by networking with specialized agencies. These could be analyzed and studied in depth. Gender auditing and development of evaluation mechanisms would also be undertaken along side.

Collection of gender disaggregated data by all primary data collecting agencies of the Central and State Governments as well as research and academic institutions in the public and private sectors would be undertaken. Data and information gaps in vital areas reflecting the status of women would be sought to be filled in by these immediately. All Ministries/Corporations/Banks and financial institutions etc would be advised to collect, collate, disseminate and maintain/publish data related to programmes and benefits on a gender disaggregated basis. This would help in meaningful planning and evaluation of policies.

7.4.2 Institutional Mechanisms: Institutional mechanisms, to promote the advancement of women, which exist at the Central and State levels, would be strengthened. This would be done through appropriate and would relate to, among others, provision of adequate resources, training and skills to effectively influence macro-policies, legislations, programmes etc. to achieve the empowerment of women.

National and State Councils would be formed to oversee the operationalisation of the Policy on a regular basis. The National Council would be headed by the Prime Minister and the State Councils by the Chief Ministers and would be broad in composition having representatives from the concerned

Departments/Ministries, National and State Commissions for Women, Social Welfare Boards, representatives of non-government organizations, women's organisations, corporate sector, trade unions, financing institutions, academics, experts and social activists. These bodies would review the progress made in implementing the Policy twice a year. The National Development Council would also be informed, from time to time, of the progress of the programme undertaken under the policy for advice and comments.

National and State Resource Centres on women would be established with mandates for collection and dissemination of information, undertaking research work, conducting surveys, implementing training and awareness generation programmes etc. These Centres would link up with Women's Studies Centres and other research and academic institutions through suitable information networking systems.

While institutions at the district level would be strengthened, women would be helped by Government at the grassroots level through its programmes to organize and strengthen self-help groups (SHGs) at the anganwadi/village/town levels. The women's groups would be helped to institutionalize themselves into registered societies and to federate at the panchyat/municipal level. These societies would bring about synergistic implementation of all the social and economic development programmes by drawing resources made available through Government and non-government channels, including banks and financial institutions and by establishing a close Interface with the panchayats/ municipalities.

7.4.3 Resource Management: Availability of adequate financial, human and market resources to implement NPEW would be managed by concerned departments, financial credit institutions and banks, private sector, civil society and other connected institutions. This process would include the following:

1. Assessment of benefits flowing to women and resource

allocation to the programmes relating to them through an exercise of gender budgeting. Appropriate changes in policies would be made to optimize benefits to women under these schemes.

2. Adequate resource allocation to develop and promote the policy outlined earlier based on (1) above by concerned Departments.
3. Developing synergy between personnel of health, rural development, education and women and child development department at field level and other village level functionaries.
4. Meeting credit needs by banks and financial credit institutions through suitable policy initiatives and development of new institutions in coordination with the Department of Women and Child Development.

The strategy of Women's Component Plan adopted in the Ninth Five Year Plan (1997-98 to 2001-02) ensuring that not less than 30 percent of benefits/funds flow to women from all Ministries and Departments would be implemented effectively so that the needs and interests of women and girls are addressed by all concerned sectors. The Department of Women and Child Development being the nodal Ministry will monitor and review the progress of the implementation of the Component Plan from time to time in terms of both quality and quantity in collaboration with the Planning Commission.

Efforts would be made to channelize private sector investments also, to support programmes and projects for advancement of women.

7.4.4 Legislation: The existing legislative structure would be reviewed and additional legislative measures taken by identified departments to implement the Policy. This would also involve a review of all existing laws including personal, customary and tribal laws, subordinate legislation, related rules as well as executive and administrative regulations to eliminate all gender discriminatory references. The process would be planned over a time period 2000-03. The specific measures required would be evolved through a consultation process involving civil society, National Commission for Women, and Department of Women and Child Development. In appropriate cases the consultation process would be widened to include other stakeholders also.

Effective implementation of legislations would be promoted by involving civil society and community. Appropriate changes in legislations would be undertaken, if necessary. In addition, following other specific measures would be taken to implement the legislation effectively:

1. Strict enforcement of all relevant legal provisions and speedy redressal of grievances would be ensured, with a special focus on violence and gender related atrocities.
2. Measures to prevent and punish sexual harassment at the place of work, protection for women workers in the organized/unorganized sector and strict enforcement of relevant laws such as Equal Remuneration Act and Minimum Wages Act would be undertaken.
3. Crimes against women, their incidence, prevention, investigation, detection and prosecution would be regularly reviewed at all crime review fora and conferences at the Central, State and District levels. Recognised, local, voluntary organizations would be authorized to lodge complaints and facilitate registration, investigations and legal proceedings related to violence and atrocities against girls and women.
4. Women's cells in police stations, women police stations, family courts, mahila courts, counselling centres, legal aid centres and nyaya panchayats would be strengthened and expanded to eliminate violence and atrocities against women.
5. Widespread dissemination of information on all aspects of legal rights, human rights and other entitlements of women, through specially designed legal literacy programmes and rights information programmes would be done.

7.4.5 Gender Sensitization: Training of personnel of executive, legislative and judicial wings of the State—with a special focus on policy and programme framers, implementation and development agencies, law enforcement machinery and the judiciary, as well as non-governmental organizations—would be undertaken. Other measures would include the following:

1. Promoting societal awareness of gender issues and women's human rights.
2. Review of curriculum and educational materials to include gender education and human rights issues.
3. Removal of all references derogatory to the dignity of women from all public documents and legal instruments.
4. Use of different forms of mass media to communicate social messages relating to women's equality and empowerment.

7.4.6 Panchayati Raj Institutions: The 73rd and 74th Amendments to the Indian Constitution have served as a breakthrough towards ensuring equal access and increased participation of women in political power structure. The PRIs would play a central role in the process of enhancing women's participation in public life. The PRIs and the local self-governments would be actively involved in the implementation and execution of NPEW the grassroots level.

7.4.7 Partnership with the Voluntary Sector Organizations: The involvement of voluntary organizations, associations, federations, trade unions, non-governmental organizations, women's organizations, as well as institutions dealing with education, training and research would be ensured in the formulation, implementation, monitoring and review of all policies and programmes affecting women. Towards this end, they would be provided with appropriate support related to resources and capacity building and facilitated to participate actively in the process of the empowerment of women.

7.4.8 International Cooperation: NPEW would aim at implementation of international obligations/commitments in all sectors on empowerment of women such as the Convention on All Forms of Discrimination Against Women (CEDAW), Convention on the Rights of the Child (CRC), International Conference on Population and Development (ICPD) and other such instruments. International, regional and sub-regional cooperation towards the empowerment of women would continue to be encouraged through sharing of experiences, exchange of ideas and technology, networking with institutions and organizations and through bilateral and multi-lateral partnerships.

Appendix

Appendix

Rural Women Workers in the Unorganized Sector: A Case Study of Bulandshahr District of Western Uttar Pradesh

---

Uttar Pradesh: A Socio-economic Overview

Uttar Pradesh is a very prominent state in India. This province was renamed as Uttar Pradesh on 26th January, 1950 when the Indian Constitution was promulgated. In the year 2000, thirteen hill districts of the state were transferred to form a new State named as Uttaranchal. In this separation, about 55 thousand sq. km. of land and about 1 crore population was transferred to Uttaranchal.

Geographical Characteristics: Total area of the State is 240928 sq. km. It is one of those states that are close to the Indo- Nepalese boarder. The State is bounded by Uttaranchal and Himachal Pradesh in the North, by Haryana in the West, by Madhya Pradesh in the North and by Bihar in the East. In the South-West, Rajasthan is its neighbour. Uttar Pradesh can be divided into two district-regions, viz.

- **Gangetic Plains:** Gangetic plains in the north: It includes the Gaga-Yamane Doab; the Ghaghra plains; the Gaga plains and the Terai. It has highly fertile alluvial soils and flat topography-(slope 2m/km.)-broken by numerous ponds, lakes and rivers.
- **Southern Hills:** The smaller Vindhya Hills and plateau regions in the south. It is characterized by hard rock strata; varied topography of hills, plains, valleys and plateau; limited availability of water.

Although the state falls in hot temperature belt, its climate varies from place to place. The climate varies because different places of the State have different heights above the main sea level. There are 3 types of seasons in the State, viz winter season, summer season and rainy season. The distribution of rainfall in the State is not uniform in all the regions. The rainfall varies from 60 cm. to 200 cm. It is worth mentioning that 93 percent of the rainfall is received by the State in the period between June to September. The remaining 7 percent rainfall is received during the winter months. Periodic failure of monsoons results in drought conditions and crop failures. In the Himalayan region, annual snow fall averaging 10 to 15 feet is common between December and March.

The soil of the State can be divided into two major categories: (a) sticky soil and (b) mixed red and black soil. In the Uttar Pradesh, the problem of soil erosion is a serious one, due to which, the fertility of large land area is being destroyed.

The major rivers of the State are: Ganges and Yamuna. Besides these, there are many small and large rivers flowing in the state. None of these rivers has its origins in the State. Other large rivers are Chambal, Ramganga, Sharda, Gomti, Kosi, Betiva and Ghagger. There are also several major canals and lakes in the State.

Though most of the mineral producing areas of the State are now in Uttaranchal, yet the State has some vital resources of minerals. Limestone, marble, diamond, gold, coal, cooper, gypsum, uranium, dolomite, selkhadi, rock-phosphate and kankar are the minerals that are found in the State.

Economic Characteristics: Uttar Pradesh (U.P.) is the second largest economy in India after Maharashtra. It is notable that:

1. The State is contributing 8.17 percent to India's GDP.
2. It is home to largest number of Small Scale unites in the country, with 12 percent of over 2.3 million units.
3. Labour efficiency is higher in UP (26) than the National Average (25).
4. State is leading manufacturer of office machinery in the country (25 percent).

Agriculture is the supporting leg of Uttar Pradesh

economy. In the State, the main occupation of the population is agriculture. The net cultivated area in the state is 168.25 lakh hectares.

There are three major types of crops sown in the state.

1. Ravi Crop: These crops include wheat, barley, peas, gram, tobacco, mustard and potato crops.
2. Kharif Crop: These crops include maize, jawar, bazra, paddy, cotton, sugarcane and oil seeds crops.
3. Zaid Crop: These crops include cucumber, tobacco, watermelon, muskmelon, onion, custard-apple and potato etc.

Uttar Pradesh is a major contributor to the national foodgrain stock. Partly this is due to the fertile regions of the Indo-Gangetic plains and partly owing to irrigation measures such as the Ganga Canal and tube-wells. Lakhimpur Kheri is a densely populated sugar producing district in the country. It is also home to 78 percent of national livestock population. It has been the most common producer of food grains in India since the 1950s due to high-yielding varieties of seed, greater availability of fertilizers and increased use of irrigation.

The agriculture contributes major part (68 percent) in the total income of the State. Moreover, the contribution of the State in wheat production of the country is more than one third (35 percent) and that of the sugarcane is slightly less than fifty percent (45 percent).

The rainfall of the State depends on monsoon. The chief sources of irrigation in the State are wells and tube-wells as about 66 percent of the total irrigated area depends upon these sources. Canal irrigation has occupied the second place.

In Uttar Pradesh, to begin with, Crop Insurance Scheme was started in 1984-1985 on the crops of wheat and rice in selected districts. Later on, it covered other crops and other districts also. The objective of the scheme is to compensate the farmer's losses due to natural calamities.

The State government is also executing other vital tasks in the field of agriculture to ensure economic growth of farmers.

Transfer of new technology of agriculture to the farmers under the Micro Management of Agriculture Scheme is an important achievement of the State Government. Under this scheme, both the male and female farmers are trained at the State, Division, District, Tehsil and Block levels, through seminars organized several times in a year.

Industry: Uttar Pradesh is one of the leading industrial States of the Country. It is understood as a leader among all the States in the case of sugar production. Handicrafts are its largest industry. Kanpur is the most industrialized city of Uttar Pradesh. In the State, textile, woollen and silk garments, agricultural implements, glass, steel, brass and other metal products, leather items, liquor, vegetable ghee, furniture, toys and many other items are manufactured by small-scale and large-scale industries at various places. Some of the items are also exported.

The garment industry has become vital to the economic development of Uttar Pradesh, providing millions of dollars in foreign exchange earnings and providing two million, mainly women, workers with a vital source of income. On one hand, the industry has enabled an increasing number of women with the opportunity to earn an income and gain independence, but there is also a dark side. Garment workers of Uttar Pradesh are facing low wages, poverty, work long hours and serious risks to their health.

The detailed description of some of the major industries in Uttar Pradesh is given below:

- **Sugar Industry:** There are about 122 sugar mills in Uttar Pradesh and nearly 50 percent of sugar being manufactured in India is manufactured in the State. In the State, Sugar mills are located at Meerut, Bareilly, Gorakhpur, Sahajahanpur, Kanpur, Allahabad, Ferozabad, Varanasi, Lucknow and Basti districts. There are 166 Cooperative cane societies in the State. Nearly 36 lakh farmers are associated with the sugar production in the state. In 2002-03, about 56.51 lakh tones of sugar was produced in the state. According to some estimates, in Uttar Pradesh, sugar production was estimated to fall by as much as 43 percent in 2008-2009, to somewhere around 5 million tonnes.

- **Textiles Industry:** Uttar Pradesh has third place in the country in the production of cotton textiles. There are 68 cotton textiles mills in the State. These mills are located at Kanpur, Ujhani, Meerut, Modinagar, Mirzapur, Etawah, Bareilly, Saharanpur, Hathras, Aligarh, Badun, Allahabad, Varanasi, and Moradabad. Kanpur is known as the Manchester of Uttar Pradesh. There are about 29 spinning mills in Uttar Pradesh.
- **Leather Industry:** Leather industry is an important export oriented industry of Uttar Pradesh. There industries are providing employment to about 3 lakh persons. Most of these employees are from scheduled and backward castes. This industry is mainly located at Agra, Meerut, Bareilly, Lucknow, and Dayalbagh. At these centres, shoes, jeans, belt, suitcases are made from leather.
- **Paper Industry:** Paper mills are located at Rampur, Lucknow and Saharanpur. Card-board is manufactured in mills located at Allahabad, Kanpur, Meerut and Saharanpur. At Meerut, cardboard is manufactured from the pulp obtained from sugarcane.
- **Glass Industry:** In Uttar Pradesh, glass industry is more developed in comparison to other states of the country. Major centres of glass industry in Uttar Pradesh are located at Firozabad, Ghaziabad, Beljor, Naini, Lucknow, Hathras, Meerut, Shikohabad, Ramnagar, Makhanpur, and Sasni. There are 90 factories in the states which manufacture glass bangles. Firozabad is the major centre for manufacturing glass bangles in India.
- **Engineering Goods Industries:** Engineering industries are also important in the State. These industries are mainly located at Kanpur, Lucknow, Rampur, Allahabad, Etawah, Noida, Meerut, Bulandshahr, Faizabad and Modinagar.

The factory located at Naini (Near Allahabad) manufactures structures of steel, hydraulic equipments, transmission towers, steel bridges, cranes etc.

- **Electronic Industry:** This industry has developed at a rapid pace in the State. The industry is mainly located at Lucknow, Allahabad, Jaunpur, Varanasi, Noida, Rai Bareily and Sahibabad. Telephone instruments are manufactured at ITI, Rai Barely.
- **Aluminium Industry:** In the state an aluminium industry located at Renu Kot (Mirzapur) manufactures aluminium sheet, and ingots. Besides it, other factories are mainly located at Agra, Aligarh, Meerut, Mathuras, Kasganj and Kanpur.
- **Vegetable oil Industry:** In the state vegetable oil (vanaspati ghee) is manufactured in factories mainly located at Kanpur, Bulandshahar, Ghaziabad, Meerut, Aligarh, Modinagar and Allahabad.
- **Chemical Industry:** In the state, major chemicals manufactured are bleaching powder, paints and varnishes, medicines, sulphuric acid, hydrochloride acid, ammonia etc. The major factories manufacturing these chemicals are located at Kanpur, Varanasi, Bareilly, Bulandshahar, Ghaziabad and Shankargarh (Allahabad).
- **Agricultural Implements and Equipment Industry:** In the state, several factories produce implements that are used is ploughing, irrigating, harvesting and planting crops. Some of these factories also manufacture equipments for processing milk and such other products. Some factories also produce equipments for transporting farm products, implements and devices protecting plants from insects etc. All these factories are mainly located at Agra, Kanpur, Aligarh, Meerut, Ghaziabad and Lucknow.
- **Other Major Industries:** Besides these industries, there are several other major industries in the State such as fertilizer industry, bicycle industry, cement industry, soap industry, silk and woollen garments industry, spirit and

liquor industry, cigarette industry, poultry Industry, water pipe industry, automobile industry etc. In addition to these, five software parks are proposed to be setup in the State. Further, it has been planned to develop 102 industrial sectors of New Okhla Industrial Development Authorities (NOIDA) by the year 2011. In Kanpur, a Software Technology Park has been set up.

Uttar Pradesh is the 'IT-Hub' of North India, with a share of software exports next to that of Karnataka. But, unlike South Indian States, IT enterprises are limited to particular areas only, like NOIDA, National Capital Region (NCR), and in the State capital-Lucknow.

Upcoming Logix Techno Park, in Noida, the largest STPI in North India. Noida is also famous for TV News, broadcasts on almost all News Channels such as Star News, Zee News, NDTV, Mahua News and several other News channels are in film city.

- **Small Scale and Cottage Industries:** The State is well known for its small scale and cottage industries since ancient times. The industries flourishing in the state are: Handicrafts, Wooden furniture and Toys, Timber, Brass, Sports goods, Biscuits, Perfumes and Scented oils, Scissors, Knives, well know handicrafts of the State are handmade cotton and silk garments, chicken-embroidered dresses, printing of envelops, carpets and durries, woollen garments and blankets and bed sheet. The small scale and cottage industries are mainly located at Meerut, Lucknow, Pilkhuwa, Mathura, Farrakhabad, Aligarh, Agra, Bareilly, Mirzapur, Muzaffarnagar, Saharanpur, Hathras, Varanasi, Moradabad, Shamli, Hapur, Ghaziabad and Kanpur.

Population: The population of the state as per census 2001 was 199.58 million. It is worth mentioning here that the contribution of the state in the total population of the country is 16.497 percent.

Transport and Communication: The efficient system of transport and communication has made effective contribution in the multifaceted development of Uttar Pradesh. There are four types of transport system available in the State.

- **Road Transport:** Uttar Pradesh has a large net work of roads. In the State, there are several National Highways, Small highways, Support Roads and Rural Roads, which connect major and minor cities, villages, and townships to one another. The total pucca road length in the State is 1,12,813 km. (2002-2003). This length includes 17,729 km. of National highway. In the year 2001-02, the number of buses under the control of State Transport Corporation was 6,33,000. Besides this, the corporation has hired private sector buses on contract basis to provide passenger transport services.
- **Railways:** In Uttar Pradesh, there is a large net work of railway lines in the plain areas. The major railway line in the State is that of Northern Railway and North-Eastern Railway. The head quarter of North-Eastern Railway is located at Gorakhpur and Lucknow in the main junction of Northern Railway. The Western Railway Zone is linked to Agra and Mathura in the State but Central Railway has its reach up to Allahabad, Kanpur and Agra. Rail cargo is handled by all the zones of Indian Railways.
- **Air Transport:** In the State, major airports are located at Amausi (Lucknow), Chakeri (Kanpur), Bawatpur (Varanasi) and Kheria (Agra). In addition to these, there are airports at Sassawa, Hindon (Ghaziabad), Rai Bareily, Jhansi, Bareilly, and Saharanpur. There is also a 'Civil Aviation Training Centre at Allahabad. Uttar Pradesh has become the first state in the country in the field of civil aviation to start its own domestic commercial flight service.
- **Water Transport:** In the State equipments and facilities are available for boat transport in the Ganges, Yamuna, Ghaggar and Gomti rivers. Besides it, boats also Churu the water of large canals of the State.

Communications: The modes of communication have

also developed in the State. Postal and telephone are the two prominent services in the State. In the state, Local, STD, Trunk and International Subscriber Dialling (ISD) services are available. Better facilities for telecommunication exercises are available in major cities of the State. Besides, Internet Cafés are also operating in almost all the small and large towns of the State. As a matter of fact, the State has become a part of the Information Technology (IT) age.

Employment: In the State, the employment to male and female workers is provided by the agricultural, industrial and various commercial and non-commercial sectors. The percentage of working population to the total population of the state is 29.7 percent. In the State, 72.2 percent of the working population is employed in the agriculture sector whereas the industrial sector provides employment only to 7.75 percent of the working population. Thus, the main occupation of the people of the State is agriculture.

The State government has launched various schemes and programmes to provide employment opportunities to the unemployed people. In the State, 'Self Employment Scheme' has also been started. The effect of all these schemes and programmes has been very positive in connecting rural and urban poor to the economic activities of the State.

Finance: The main heads of income of the State are taxes and duties levied by the State Government and the share of the State in taxes and duties levied by the Union Government. In addition, the State Government also receives statutory and other grants as well as loans and advances from the central government for various development and non-development purposes. The share of non-taxes and duties in the incomes of the State is, however, very small.

The State Government incurs expenditure on agriculture and allied activities, animal husbandry, fisheries, forests, industries, transport and communication, education, medical facilities, power and water supply, irrigation, floor and pollution control, rural development, welfare work of scheduled castes, scheduled tribes and backward castes, health and family welfare, sports, mines, payment of interest on loans and advances and loan redemption, public administration, grants to local bodies, community services, food and civil supply, justice, services and technology, tourism etc.

As the expenditure of the State Government is more than its receipts, it leaves a fiscal deficit.

Education: Children's education in India can be greatly improved. At present extremely high levels of Children are not attending schools and instead of enjoying the basic right to learn and Grow are forced to work under very harsh and inhuman conditions.

Every child should have the right to learn and get a basic education, and more importantly that every child should be treated with love and respect.

The State Government has made sincere efforts to make the education easily available to the students. According to the Directive Principles of State Policy of our Constitution, there is a provision for imparting education to every child up to 14 years of age. The efforts are being made to implement it in the State.

As per Census 2001, the total literacy rate in the State was 57.36 percent only. Thus, for the overall development of education in the State, total literacy programme was started from 1991. This programme has to be implemented in all the 70 district of the State in three stages as follows:

No. of districts covered under total Literacy Campaign	16
No. of districts to be covered under Higher Literacy Programme	30
No. of districts approved under Continuous Education	25
Total number of districts	71

The education imparted in the State can be divided into three groups:

- **Primary Education:** The State Government has established Government Primary Schools and there are also recognized private primary schools for imparting education up to 5th class to the children from the age of 6 to 14 years. In the cities and sub-cities of the State, English medium schools are also run by the private managements. The State Government provides grant to promote primary schools every year. In the Budget for 2006-07, the State Government made a provision of ₹ 21,884.95 lakh for grants to non-government primary schools under the planned expenditure and of ₹ 3,24,993.23 lakh under the non-planned expenditure.

- **Intermediate Education:** The intermediate education in the State is looked after by the Director, Intermediate Education, Allahabad. For the successful implementation at the State and the District levels, directives are issued from time to time. The Board of Intermediate Education conducts High School and Intermediate examination through various centres in Uttar Pradesh. In the Budget for 2006-07, the State Government provided ₹ 1,90,005 lakh for grant to non-government intermediate colleges under the non-planned expenditure and ₹ 3,519.55 lakh under the planned expenditure. The state government has also established government high schools and intermediate colleges in urban and rural areas.
- **Higher Education:** Higher education has, as a matter of fact, played an important role in the growth of the State in the fields of Science, culture, economic, and social spheres. The Directorate of Higher Education (U.P) which is located at Allahabad looks after the tasks related to higher education. The State government provides financial assistance to State Universities and the affiliated colleges. In the state both the government and non-government colleges are engaged in imparting higher education to the students. The degree and post-graduate college which are

working under the self-financing scheme is not given grant in aid by the State government. In the state, regional offices have been established by the Government for financial control on colleges and for solving their problems.

Apart from the facilities for general education in the State, there are several technical and medical colleges which impart education in their fields of specialisation.

- **Technical Education:** Rapid industrialisation of the state has encouraged technical education in wider perspective. The Department of Technical Education, (U.P.) is making constant efforts to increase the quality of technical training and to bring technical training in tune with the contemporary needs. There is a large number of State and aided polytechniques, special institutes, major research institutes and institutes for imparting training in art, culture and music.
- **Medical Education:** Medical education and training is the activity of medical and health department. This department provides various services which includes medical treatment, health services and family welfare. Out of medical colleges in the State, two are being operated by the Union Government. There are J.L. Nehru Medical College, Aligarh and Institute of Medical Sciences, Varanasi.

  The State government has been making consistent efforts to provide education in ayurvedic, unani and homoeopathic medicines through the colleges established in the State.
- **Other Educational Programmes:** The State Government has also established 'Uttar Pradesh Rajarishi Tandon Open University' to spread education among the masses.

  A programme of unorganised education to provide education to children, who leave schools on account of poverty or domestic problems, is conducted by the State Government. Such children are imparted education at their houses. This programme is being conducted in those areas where literacy level is low and the area is academically backward.

Several vocational programmes are being conducted in the State to educate adults in rural areas. Women of rural areas are also being educated in the concepts of family welfare, family planning, maternity, child education and rural occupations.

The State Government has also started a scheme for imparting vocational education to students at the intermediate level.

Caste System: Caste system in the State plays an important role in almost all walks of life. Castes have some general characteristics. However, the advent of the new era and modernisation of the State have led to the improvement of their living conditions, behaviour, thinking, education etc. Besides the upper castes, schedule castes, schedule tribes and other backward castes also thrive in the state. The socio-cultural characteristics of these castes and tribes have remained intact. Their economic conditions are, however, not satisfactory. There are 66 major scheduled castes, 79 backward castes and 6 scheduled tribes in the state. The State government is implementing various programmes for their welfare. Social Welfare Department was set up in U.P. in February, 1955 to achieve the following objectives:

1. To help the comparatively backward sections of the society.
2. To implement the various social welfare tasks on the basis of modern principles and systems.

The State Government has initiated many welfare schemes for the welfare scheduled castes, scheduled tribes and backward castes. Such schemes can be divided into five types of programmes and plans such as: (a) educational; (b) economic; (c) social; (d) health; and (e) housing. The objective of all these schemes is the all round development of those people of the society who have been backward and ignored.

Social Welfare Schemes: In order to educate and rehabilitate the blind, deaf and dumb children, schools are being run by the State government. The State government has also managed two schools at Lucknow and Allahabad to train and educate mentally retarded children. The physically disabled and handicapped persons and children are educated in two schools, one each at Pratapgarh and Lucknow.

To give comfort to old and weak persons two residential houses are being managed in the State, one of them is in Lucknow (for men) and other one is in Varanasi district (for women).

The women and child development department was created in March, 1989 for the welfare of women and children. The objective of department is to integrate and monitor programmes being implemented by various departments for their welfare. A Mahila Ashram has also been established in Kanpur district to give protection to the humiliated and abused women. These women are trained in many handicrafts and skills so that they may be self dependent. The scheme for providing financial assistance to women tortured by the dowry custom was initiated in 1990-91.

The State government is conducting various schemes for helpless infants and children. A nutrition home is being managed in Lucknow to give shelter to destitute and abandoned infants in the age group of 0 to 6 years. In order to look after abandoned and orphan infants, 6 centres have been established by the State Government. Moreover, in order to provide dwellings, education and training to these infants and children, child centres (Bal Sadan) have been established in the State.

The state government gives subsistence grant to such widows of the society that are ignored, abandoned and without any support. Widows are also given training in weaving for one year at Destitute Widow Weaving Training Centres. In order to rehabilitate the trainees one weaving machine is given free of cost to each one of them after the completion of the training period.

Under the Immoral Trafficking Act (1950), the State government has established District Shelter and Entrance Homes to give shelter to morally troubled women. They are given free food, clothes and lodging facilities.

The State government started a scheme in 1991-92 to give prize to a person who marries a widow of less than 35 year of age. A prize of ₹ 11,000 is given to such married couple. There are also several other schemes and programmes to provide employment to SCs, STs and OBCs and women. Other schemes have also been started in the State to provide training to rural youth for employment.

Language: Hindi is the mother tongue of the State. The other languages which are also frequently spoken in the State are Urdu and English. The State government has taken various steps to promote Urdu language at the primary, junior high school and at the secondary levels. The state government established State Education Research and Training Board in 1981. Two departments of this board are actively engaged in improving the quality of languages spoken in the State. The State government has also taken steps to develop various regional Indian languages which are spoken in the State.

Social Relations: The poor people in the State have failed to interact adequately with the other strata of the society. Their activities are restricted to their own circles. Age old social repression has developed inferiority complex in them. Thus, it has not been possible to remove social inequality. The poor masses in the State consider themselves more as victims rather than equally important partners in work. The rich people in the state are convinced that they derive their high social status from the ownership of their land, property and wealth. They feel that they provide jobs to the poor workers. The story of exploitation continues with a different shade and social transformation in favour of the poor has failed to take off.

Social impact, to a very great extent, is the result of economic impact. If a community or class is economically sound, it is expected that it would be socially well also. The two aspects are generally, positively correlated. However, the various programmes, run by the government to educate and provide employment to poor men and women in the state have generated greater confidence among them. It has also brought about some changes in their outlook. But so far as the social relations are concerned, rich people show no liberal attitude towards the economically weaker people.

Western Uttar Pradesh

From economic point of view, the State has been divided into 4 regions namely Western Region, Central Region, Eastern Region and Bundelkhand Region. Western Region of Uttar Pradesh includes the following 26 districts:

Saharanpur, Bulandshahr, Meerut, Ghaziabad, Muzaffarnagar, Aligarh, Mathura, Agra, Mainpuri, Etah, Bareilly, Bijnor, Badaun, Moradabad, Shahjahanpur, Pilibhit, Rampur, Farukhabad, Etawah, Firozabad, Gautambudh Nagar, Hathras, Jyotibafulle Nagar, Kannoj, Baghpat and Aureyya.

The total geographical area of western region of the state is 79956 sq. km., which is 36.7 percent of the total geographical area of the state. The climate of this region varies from place to place though it is predominantly hot. In this region winter, summer and rainy seasons are found. The highest hot temperature is found in Agra and the lowest in Bareilly. The average rainfall in this region hovers between the values of 60 cm. to 100cm. The rainy season is comparatively short in Western region. The soil in this region is predominantly dark brown. In the district of Saharanpur, Muzaffarnagar and Meerut, the soil is fertile. The Ganga and Yamuna are the most important rivers in this region. Ramganga and Hindon rivers are also significant in this region. There are also some lakes and canals in the region.

Agriculture: The Western region of Uttar Pradesh is

mainly an agricultural region. In this region there major types of crops such as Ravi, Kharif and Jayed are grown. The major crops of this region are: wheat, barley, peas, gram, arhar, potato, mustard, maize, jawar, bajra, paddy, cotton, sugarcane, oilseeds, tobacco, onion and watermelon. Among the foodgrain crops wheat crop is the most important crop followed by the rice and maize crops. In other crops, sugarcane and potato crops are the most important crops that are grown in this region.

The chief modes of irrigation in this region are tube wells and wells. However, canal water is also used for irrigation.

Industry: Western region of the state is famous for certain industrial products. The sugar is manufactured in this region in the districts of Meerut, Muzaffarnagar, Bareilly and Shahjahanpur.

In this region, paper mills are located at Meerut, Rampur and Saharanpur. Cardboard is also manufactured in mills located at Meerut and Saharanpur.

The region also produces vegetable oil (vanaspati ghee). It is manufactured in factories that are located at Ghaziabad, Meerut, Modinagar and Aligarh.

The major centres of leather industries in this region are Agra, Dayalbagh, Meerut, Bareilly. At these centres shoes, jeans, belts, and suitcases are made from leather.

This region is also famous for the production of match sticks. These are produced in Bareilly, Saharanpur, Rampur and Meerut.

Cotton textile industry is also important in this region. The major mills of this industry are located at Modinagar, Etawah, Bareilly, Meerut, Hathras, Aligarh, Saharanpur, Moradabad and Badaun. The major silk garment mills are located in Modinagar and Etawah.

The modern major edible oil mills in this region are located at Agra, Modinagar, Bulandshahar and Ghaziabad.

Glass industry is a very prominent industry of western Uttar Pradesh. The major centres of this region are located at

Firozabad, Ghaziabad, Hathras, Meerut, Sasni, Ramnagar and Shikohabad, Firozabad is the major centre for manufacturing glass bangles in India.

There are Aluminium factories also in this region which manufacture various aluminium products. These factories are predominantly located in Agra, Aligarh, Meerut and Mathura.

Electronics industry has also developed in this region at a rapid rate. Its factories are mainly located at Noida and Sahibabad.

There are many other major factories in Western region of Uttar Pradesh that manufacture agricultural equipments and implements of various types. In this region these factories are chiefly located at Agra, Aligarh, Meerut and Bareilly.

In the Western Region chemical industries that manufacture medicines, paints, varnishes, sulphuric acid, ammonia etc. are mainly located at Bareilly and Ghaziabad.

In the western region industries which produce soaps are mainly located at Agra, Modinagar, Ghaziabad, Bulandshahar, Meerut and Muzaffarnagar.

In the western region the factories that manufacture spirit and liquor are chiefly located at Mohannagar (Ghaziabad), Saharanpur, Meerut and Rampur.

Cigarette industry is also located in this region at Ghaziabad and Saharanpur. Other industries such as water pipe industry is mainly located at Ghaziabad, china potteries industry at Khurja and Ghaziabad, tine canes industry at Agra, Hathras, Ghaziabad, Etawah, and Mainpuri and sport goods industry at Meerut, Ghaziabad and Saharanpur.

The small-scale and cottage industries are also located in this region which manufacture handicrafts, wooden furniture, timber and brass goods, biscuits, perfumes, scissors, knives, cotton clothes, handmade garments, chicken and embroideries dresses, printing of cards and envelopes, carpets woollen garments and blankets and pan masalas.

The districts of Saharanpur, Ghaziabad, Bareilly, Bulandshahar and Hathras are major producers of wooden furniture. Brass industries that make alloys are mainly located at Farukhabad, Moradabad, Hapur and Shamli. Brass locks are mainly manufactured at Aligarh, Knives and scissors mainly at Rampur, Hathras, Aligarh, Mathura and Meerut. Iron weights are chiefly manufactured at Meerut and Agra and Saharanpur.

The major large industries operating in the western region of Uttar Pradesh are:

1. Oil refinery factory at Mathura.
2. Bharat Electrical Industry at Ghaziabad.
3. Atomic Plant at Narora (Bulandshahr).

Population: The population of Western Region of Uttar Pradesh as per Census of 2001 is 6.11 crore which is 36.4 percent of the total population of the State. The highest population in the region resides at Moradabad district (37.48lakh) followed by Agra district (36.11 lakh), Bareilly district (35.99 lakh) and Muzaffarnagar district (35.41 lakh).

The Western Region is dominated by upper Castes. Scheduled castes and backward castes also reside in this region in sufficient number. The density of population of western region is 764 per sq. km. The number of females in this region is 865 per thousand of males.

Employment: In the Western region, the employment to the working population is mainly provided by agriculture and allied sectors. It has been estimated that about 70 percent of the working population of the region is employed in these sectors. The big small-scale industries and commercial and business establishments also provide employment to about 20 percent of the total population and the remaining 10 percent is employed in miscellaneous works such as domestic works, construction work, self-employment works etc.

Transport and Communication: An efficient transport system in the Western region has made effective contribution towards the development of the region. All the four types of transport system namely road, rail, water and air exist in this region. Road transport provides efficient services in the region, which includes express and long distance services, dial-up services, fair services, city transport services, night transport services etc. There is also a large network of railway lines in western region of Uttar Pradesh. In this region the Northern railway zone has many branches which connect small and large cities. The Western railway zone is limited to Agra and Mathura, Khaira (Agra) is one of the major airports of the State.

The modes of communication have also developed in Western Uttar Pradesh. Postal and Telephone services are the prominent services. The Local, STD, Trunk and ISD (International Subscription Dial-up) services are also available in Western Uttar Pradesh. Internet Cafes are also operating in this region.

The total length of pucca road in this region is 32,277 km. which is 36 percent of the pucca roads in the State.

Finance and Earnings: Western region of Uttar Pradesh is a prosperous region. Thus, it provides sufficient finances to the State Government. Moreover, per capita income of the people of this region as compared to the other regions of the State is also more.

The Western region of Uttar Pradesh is quite advance in the matter of education. The education in this region is provided at the primary, intermediate and higher levels and also training in education at various levels. The literacy rate as per census 1991, in this region was 42 percent. It was 54.8 percent in case of males and 26.6 percent in case of females.

The State Government is sincerely trying to increase education facilities up to the intermediate level in the Western region. As regards the position of universities and colleges affiliated to them, it is noticeable that there are 3 academic universities namely, B.R. Ambedkar University, Agra, Ch. Charan Singh University, Meerut and Mahatma Jyotibaphulle Rohilkhand University, Bareilly. There is also one Central University at Aligarh named as Aligarh Muslim University, Aligarh.

In this region, there are several diploma level

Politechniques. There are two State Government Medical colleges in this region situated at Agra and Meerut. There is also a private medical college at Ghaziabad duly recognized by the Medical Council of India, New Delhi. In the field of medical education, there are ayurvedic and unani, homoeopathic and dental colleges in Western Uttar Pradesh.

Bulandshahr District

The history of Bulandshahr begins even before 1200 B.C. This region is nearer to the capital of Pandavas-Indraprasth and Hastinapur. After of decline of Hastinapur, Ahar which is situated in the north east of district Bulandshahr became an important place for Pnadavas. With passes of time the king Parma made a fort on this part of region and a king named Ahibaran laid the foundation of a tower called Baran (Bulandshahr). Since it was perched on a highland it came to be known as high city which was translated into passion language as Bulandshahr. At present, this is called by this name.

The ancient ruins found at places Bhatora Veerpur, Ghalibpur etc. are symbolic of antiquity of Bulandshahr. There are several other important places in the District from where statues of medieval age and objects of ancient temples had been founded. Even today several historical and ancients objects such as coins, inscriptions etc. are preserved in Lucknow State Museum.

Geographical Situation: The District of Bulandshahr is in Meerut region of Utter Pradesh located between Ganga and Yamuna rivers. This is situated between 28.4 ^{0} south and 28.0^0 north latitude and between 77.0 ^{0} and 78.0 ^{0} longitudes.

The District is about 84 km. in length and 62 km. is breadth. The district is situated 237.44 meters above the sea level.

The river Ganga in the East separates this District from Moradabad and Badaun Districts and in the West river Yamuna separates the District from Haryana state and Delhi.

In the North, the District is Ghaziabad and in the South-East are the borders of Aligarh District.

The total population of the District as per Census 2001 is 30,09,860 lakh, in which number of females to males ration was 879:1000. The overall literacy rate as per Census in 2001 was 59.5 percent—males 74 percent and females 42.5 percent.

The total area of district is 4352 sq km., which is about 1.48 percent of the total area of U.P.

The total number of Tehsil in the district is Seven located at Dibai, Anoopshahr, Khurja, Shikarpur, Siyana, Bulandshahr and Sikandrabad. The total number of Development Blocks in this district is sixteen located at Bulandshahr, Gulaathi, Dibai, Lakhaowati, Shikarpur, Khurja, Pahasu, Arniya, Sikandrabad, Anoopshar, Danpur, Siyana, B.B Nagar, Jhagirabad, Uncha Gaon, and Agauta.

In the district the informal sector has largely been due to migration of people from rural areas to urban areas. The motive behind such a migration is employment opportunities in urban areas. The initial temptation to migration generally comes from the organized or formal sector in manufacturing, administrative, commercial and other allied establishments. These establishments however, failed to absorb large labour force due to less demand from these sectors. But the surplus labour, which could not get entry in the formal sector, was absorbed to a major extent by the rest of the urban economy which is termed as the informal sector. This position is still prevailing in the urban areas of the district.

The rural area of Bulandshahr district was chosen for deep and wide investigation. The characteristics of the informal sector in the district are:

Casual Nature of Employment: Lack of permanent nature of employment is the basic characteristic of informal sector in this district. The casual employment to the workers is mainly provided in manufacturing units, commercial establishments, agricultural, operations and allied works and construction work. Employment of women in the sampled area is getting increasing casualised. The employers recruit women as casual workers in order to minimize the financial burden.

Women Workers-Illiterate and Ignorant: In the study area women workers are not only illiterate but are ignorant also. Whatever skills have been acquired by some of them is outside the formal school system. Without any job experience, they enter as new entrants.

Small Size of Establishments: In the district small establishments employ casual workers with no job security. The size of employment in these establishments is very small. There is a single worker in some of the self-employed establishments. Local inputs are mostly used by these establishments because of small sector operations.

Family Ownership of Enterprises: There is no structural organization in family ownership enterprises in the district. It has been observed that in many cases, the head of the family or a member of the family does the work himself with the help of other members of the family. In these enterprises there is neither an employee nor an employer.

Traditional Technology: The informal sector in the district uses indigenous technology of production which is a labour intensive and low level technology. As these production-units are very small, they do not have enough financial resources to put modern technology at the desired level. The old technology is cheaper for them.

Unhygienic Conditions of Work: The working conditions of informal sector workers in the district are miserable. In most of the work places there is no sufficient ventilation and natural light. Thus, the workers suffer from eye strain. In some cases they do not have proper sitting arrangements. Thus, there are no minimum facilities at work place. The workers under these conditions are exposed to several health hazards.

Low Wages: In the district the informal sector workers are paid very low wages. In this matter, women workers are differentiated from men workers as they are paid much less than their counter parts even for the same work. In most of the cases the contractors assume wage rate determination as they directly recruit the workers. In such cases contractors ensure a higher margin of remuneration for themselves.

Lack of Workers' Unions: In the district there are no trade unions of informal sector workers. Thus, they always live with uncertainty of not knowing how much would be available and when. Lack of organization or unions hampers the bargaining power of both men and women workers and their power to resist exploitation. The workers, therefore, suffer as they have no voice to put their grievances before the employers.

Long Hours of Work: In Bulandshahr district, the working hours of informal sector workers are not fixed. Sometimes, they work for long duration i.e. from 9 to 12 hours continuously and there are no regular holidays for them. For women workers, there are no crèche facilities for their young and nursing children. The status and quality of life of women workers has worsened due to dual work-house hold work and work at the employment place.

Exploitation and Harassment of Workers: In Bulandshahr district, the employers exploit the women workers. These workers also face ill treatment from the employers. It was reported by the women workers that their children were also exploited, especially their daughters. In some cases sexual harassment with domestic women workers was reported. Rural women and girls who become domestic for families are no more than slaves are, while at work, they are paid negligible pay and provided with very low quality of food. In most cases daughters are rarely sent to schools because they help their mothers at work and home.

Lack of Safety and Security: There is no system of social security on which informal sector workers can fall back. The position of women workers in the district is worst in this matter. The women labour force is particularly excluded from social security benefits as the nature of their employment is casual or on daily wages or on piece rate.

Sampled Area

In this study, both primary and Secondary data have been used to examine the role of working women engaged in informal sector in Bulandshahr district.

Primary data were collected with the help of questionnaire cum schedules which were prepared for this purpose. For sampling purposes, the area of the district was divided into two parts viz. rural and urban. For taking the representation of rural women workers in the informal sector the villages of the district of Bulandshahr were chosen for drawing a sample of villages and women respondents. A special survey of the area was conducted for this purpose. In view of resources, it was decided to restrict the survey up to 5 percent villages of different Development Blocks. The number of inhibited villages in the development blocks is 1175. Out of these development blocks 59 Villages were selected for study.

Findings, Conclusions and Suggestions

The economic participation of women workers in the district is very important. In the district vast majority of women are employed in agricultural sector. Amongst rural women workers, about 85 percent are employed in agriculture sector as labourers. Survey of the area has shown that two third of agricultural operations are performed by women. These women participate in agricultural operations besides the houschold works. Generally, rural women workers are hired by rich cultivators on daily wage basis.

The small manufacturing units in the district have also employed women in various types of jobs. They are, however, employed in simple production processes. The small manufacturing units which produce pottery, cotton clothes including Khadi clothes, silk and woollen garments, handicrafts, toys, perfumes and scented oils, biscuits, sarees, ladies dresses, furniture etc. have employed women workers in their establishments. These, women are mostly employed temporarily on piece rate wages. Besides manufacturing units, women workers are also employed in hospitals and nursing homes and in trading and commercial establishments in urban areas of the district. In the district, a large number of women workers are also employed in the building and construction sector. These women workers are assigned the work of carrying earth, mortar, cement, stones, water, bricks, etc., which they carry on their heads or backs. They are also employed for crushing the stones, carrying head-loads and for working on hand pumps etc. The women workers in construction work are employed as they are cheaper than men and are found more disciplined.

The domestic service is also an important occupation particularly for migrated women in urban and semi-urban areas of the district. The employers of women domestic servants are mainly the businessmen, doctors, engineers, chartered accountants, teachers, government employees and other high economic strata families. These women are either full time workers, part time workers or residential workers. The women domestic servants are assigned various jobs such as cooking, cleaning utensils, washing clothes, cleaning the house, fetching water, bringing vegetables and provisions from the market etc. The wages paid to the women workers sometimes include the labour of their daughters. These young girls are not given cash for the work that they perform with their mothers.

The self-employment is regarded as one of the important unorganised sector occupations. In Bulandshahr district, a large number of women in urban and semi-urban areas are self-employed. Most of them are vendors, hawkers and petty businessmen. Artisan work is also included in self-employment activities such as handicraft production and household enterprises like knitting, weaving etc. In urban areas women run roadside water and tea stalls and vegetable and fruit shops. They are also engaged in street vending, retailing in cotton and woollen garments, second-hand clothes, utensils, toys, petty grocers etc. The women in the district also work as dry cleaners, pressers, washers, tailors etc. In the cities of Bulandshahr, Khurja and Anoopshahr women are also running beauty parlours. The women hawkers on the streets of urban and semi-urban residential areas of the district who sell flowers, vegetables, fruit, ready foods, toys, clothes etc. are very prominent.

The unorganised sector in Bulandshahr district is characterised by the several factors such as wage discrimination between men and women, no limit of minimum wages, long hours of work, lack of job security, lack of legislative cover, lack of minimum facilities at work place, heavy physical work, ill treatment by the employers and sexual harassment and exploitation.

All building sites had the statutory obligation to provide crèches for young children of women workers. But in the study area they were not provided did not find them anywhere. Mothers bring their children to sites and put them up near the work places. There they lay often covered with dust and the chips of materials used, with flies settling on their faces. Older children looked after the younger ones; the mother kept an eye on them and visited them on and off. Although the standards for safety are prescribed, the sites in general, did not display warning signs of any kind, nor was there fencing of dangerous places, trap holes, heights, etc.

The concept of economic participation of women workers is playing a very crucial role in economic life throughout the world. The empirical study of economic participation of women workers in unorganised sector in Bulandshahr district is based on 320 respondents randomly selected from the study area for each sector. The findings of the survey of the study area have revealed the following specific features of the unorganised sector in the district:

1. The women workers engaged in unorganized sector are mostly elder adolescents in the age group of 25 to 45 years.

2. The working hours of these women workers are generally 8 to 9 hours a day.
3. About 51 percent of the working women belong to backward castes and 35 percent to scheduled castes. The involvement of upper castes women is about 9 percent and of schedules tribe women is about 5 percent in the unorganised sector.
4. The percentage of illiterate working women is about 27 percent and that of having low level of literacy is 60 percent, lack .of awareness among women workers is general. Due to illiteracy or low level education they are unaware of their demand nationally/internationally.

Rural Women Enjoying Literacy Programme:

1. In the unorganised sector the working women are discriminated in wage payment as compared to male workers. The women workers are paid about 30 percent less wages for doing the same work.
2. The involvement of women workers in this sector is 50 percent due to the need of helping the family members and 30 percent owing to their poverty. In miscellaneous causes, the burden of debts is important.
3. The attitude of the employers towards these women workers is generally unsympathetic. Some changes have, however, taken place in their attitude in recent years.
4. 90 percent of women workers are not provided adequate facilities at work places. In some cases even the toilets have not been separately provided to female workers. In most of the cases there is no crèche facility for their nursing children.

Childcare is the Biggest Issue:

1. 100 percent of women worker face the problem of job insecurity and 90 percent of the excess burden of work.
2. About 95 percent of the working women are appointed on temporary or casual basis for a very limited period, which ranges from a day to a week or a fortnight. Permanent appointments are very rare.

3. 99 percent of the working women are not provided leave with wages/pay, medical facilities, regular holidays and maternity benefits.

Medical Facilities for Rural Women:

1. About 3 percent of women workers have suffered from sexual harassments by the employers. However, almost all women workers are exploited in some way or the other. The middlemen are also involved in their exploitation. These women do not lodge complaints to any authority against their exploitation or harassment due to fear of losing the job or work.
2. As there is no organization of women workers, they do not have the bargaining capacity regarding wage and terms and condition of appointment. In their cases the proverb that "Beggars and not choosers" applies. There is a need for government and NGOs intervention to uplift the skills of the artisans and also empower them with marketing and production skills.
3. Women workers are not aware of the provisions enforced by government through various Acts to protect their interests.
4. The need to bring in awareness to the rural women about loan and schemes, workshops provided by the government.

Rural women have to be empowered to face the ever increasing demand for their products and also threats posed by the multinational corporations.

Like women's unpaid domestic work, women's home based productive work for cash income is generally invisible and undervalued. This is very paradoxical because income derived from home based work by women frequently provides the basis for the survival of families in poverty. As we have seen above, this is primarily an unorganised sector, falling under the small-scale and cottage industry category. It is, therefore, generally ignored by data gathering systems, policy makers and administrators.

The policy of the government with regard to women workers is to strengthen their bargaining capacity, to improve their wages and to open up better employment opportunities for them. Besides, the Factories Act, 1948, the Minimum Wages Act, 1948, The Employees Insurance Act, 1948, and the Payment of Bonus Act, 1965 have also been enacted. To safeguard their interests in employment, however, two more acts have been specifically enacted for them. These are (i) the Maternity Benefit Act, 1961 and the Equal Remuneration Act, 1976.

The Government of India and the Uttar Pradesh Government have started various schemes and programmes for the employment of workers of weaker sections of the society, which include female workers also. The Integrated Rural Development Programme (IRDP) was implemented for the socio-economic development of rural communities. Its aim is to eradicate rural poverty, to generate more income for the poor sections of rural society and to create substantial opportunities of employment. This programme aimed at integration of five major sectors viz., agriculture, village cottage and small-scale industries, tertiary sectors, employment in various services and labour mobilization training in skills and organized mobility to tie up labour with opportunity. This programme has been implemented in all the 5300 Development Blocks of the country.

Another programme named as Training Rural Youth for Self-Employment (TRYSEM) was started on 15th August, 1979 with the objective of equipping rural youth with necessary skills and technological know-how to make them capable to seek self-employment in agriculture and allied activities, industries, services and business activities. Only the youth belonging to the families of the target groups of small and marginal farmers, agricultural labourers, rural artisans and others below the poverty line who are normally between the ages of 18 and 35 years are eligible. This scheme provides that 50 percent of the youth selected for training must be from scheduled caste/scheduled tribe families and minimum 40 percent should be women among the total trainees. A suitable stipend up to ₹ 300 per month and free tool-kit worth about ₹ 600 is given to each trainee. In 1979-80, this scheme was started in all the Development Blocks of the state.

A scheme known as Development of Women and Children in Rural Areas (DWCRA) was taken up in 1982. This scheme aimed at improving the status and living conditions of women by increasing their income and also to provide support services needed to enable them to take up income generating activities. Under this scheme women and children are in focus in services like welfare, health, nutrition and education.

Jawahar Rozgar Yojana (JRY) was launched in the last year of the Seventh Five Year Plan (1989-90). The primary objective of the scheme is to provide employment to the unemployed members of those families that are living in the rural areas below the poverty line. Generation of additional employment or productive work has also been the objective of the scheme. In providing employment preference is given to SCs/STs. Under the scheme 30 percent employment has been reserved for women. Although the programme has made some headway in providing employment but the target of providing 90-100 days of employment for every registered person has not been achieved.

Swarnajayanti Gram Swarozgar Yojana (SGSY) was launched in 1999 as a self-employment programme for the rural masses. The objective of the programme is to promote the micro enterprises and to bring the assisted poor families above the poverty line. Among the rural poor, the SGSY has special focus on vulnerable groups. Accordingly, SCs/STs would account for at least 50 percent of the Swarozgaries, women for 40 percent and the disabled for 3 percent. The programme seeks to promote multiple credit rather than one time credit.

Sampoorna Grameen Rozgar Yojana (SGRY) was launched in September, 2001 to provide additional wage employment in rural areas. The programme lays special emphasis on women, scheduled castes, schedules tribes and parents of children withdrawn from hazardous employment.

Another scheme, Nehru Rozgar Yojana (NRY) was launched in 1989. It caters to the economic needs of the urban poor, mainly unemployed and underemployed, by providing the employment opportunities through skills up-gradation assistance in setting up their own micro-enterprises and scheme for shelter and housing up-gradation.

In addition to the above schemes, Swarna Jayanti Shahri Rozgar Yojana (SJSRY) was approved in 1997 to implement Urban Self-Employment Programme (USEP) and Urban Wage Employment Programme (UWEP).

A Special Employment Scheme was implemented by the Khadi and Gramodyog Board in Uttar Pradesh for training in New Model Charkhas and Self-Employment. This scheme is being implemented for the women of Scheduled Castes, Schedules Tribes, minorities and weaker sections living in rural areas of the State. The objective of this scheme is to arrange work for these women at their homes and effect qualitative improvement.

Ambedkar Vishesh Rozgar Yojana (AVRY) has been implemented by the Government of Uttar Pradesh with the objective of implementing plans for generating employment, to create opportunities for continuous employment and to increase the incomes of rural families.

Besides the above mentioned schemes, a special employment scheme, the National Rural Employment Guarantee Programme (NREGP) Act was launched on February 2, 2006, after passing the National Rural Employment Guarantee Act (NREGA) in September 2005 by the Prime Minister, Dr. Manmohan Singh. A distinguishing feature of the NREGA is that it provides the legal right of employment and has the potential to generate more employment directly and indirectly as also to transform the rural economy. This scheme is now known as Mahatma

Gandhi National Rural Employment Guarantee Act (MGNREGA).

The MGNREGA has been designed as a safety net to reduce migration by rural poor households in the lean period by providing them at least a hundred days of guaranteed work to unskilled manual labour on demand at minimum wages as prescribed by the respective States. The adult member of every household, who resides in the rural area and is willing to do unskilled manual work, may apply for registration of the household for issuance of job card. Registration is made for a period of five years and may be renewed from time to time. Employment must be provided to all applicants within fifteen days of receipt of an application and within a radius of five kms from their place of residence. In case, employment cannot be provided within fifteen days of receipt of the application, the applicant shall be entitled to a daily unemployment allowance.

It is a fact that the process of westernization started after the independence of the country. The development made after this changed the whole order of the society. This has changed the traditional position of the Indian Women also. The women have also started to play a direct economic role as wage earners in various works. Though, the proportion of women in unorganised sector has increased but there is still discrimination against them in employment. The main reason of discrimination is that there is no organization of working women in the district.

Suggestions: It is discouraging to note that despite the implementation of various Acts, Schemes and Programmes, to improve the lot of working women, the practical side of their implementation and their results in terms of desired impact are very dismal. An analysis of close observations at various levels and personal interviews and discussions with women workers has focused several handicaps and difficulties that have hindered to safeguard their interests in employment and social set-up.

Thus, the following steps are suggested to improve the economic and social life of women workers in the district:

1. Illiteracy, ignorance, lack of vocational skill has resulted in exploitation, harassment and torture of women workers. Thus, serious efforts should be made to provide educational opportunity, awareness and vocational training to women workers. The State must take special care to reach women in unorganised sector. The State must endeavour to take education at their doorsteps. This education should not merely be for literacy but it should be skill imparting. The government should be careful that the schemes and programmes reach the targeted groups. The education to working women should be provided according to their requirements and should simultaneously uplift their socio-economic awareness. The curriculum for the education of women should be such as to lessen beliefs in rituals. Thus, the education must, promote a rational and scientific attitude of women.
2. Many research studies have shown that participation of rural women has increased in education and sports activities.
3. The discrimination of women workers in wage payment and terms and conditions of work should be discarded. The principle of equal pay for equal work should be effectively enforced. The labour laws and schemes, which protect the interests of women workers, should be very carefully and forcefully implemented. The cases of violation of these laws must be strictly dealt with and punished. This step will help to safeguard the interests of women workers and at the same time discourage the discrimination in employment against them.
4. No improvement in the economic life of women workers will come unless their exploitation and harassment is stopped. The exploiters and middlemen should be eliminated. The women workers should be encouraged by the social workers to fight against their exploitation or

harassment. The concerned authorities should be approached by the women workers for the redressal of their grievances.

5. The provision of adequate facilities for the women workers at the workplaces must be ensured. The separate toilets for female workers and crèches for their young and nursing children should be provided at all workplaces. The machinery enforcing the labour laws in the district should see that minimum facilities at workplaces are provided by the employers and in cases of default action against them should be taken according to the provisions of the labour laws in this respect.

Sanitary, Crèche Facilities Must for Women

1. The women workers should be ensured of limited working hours. They should also be given weekly rest with pay/wages, maternity benefits, regular holidays and medical facilities. The district administration should carefully ensure that these facilities are provided to the women workers. These facilities will improve the working efficiency of these women workers, which will directly or indirectly benefit the employers also.
2. The problems of getting credit are big one for these women workers. Due to burden of family members and poverty, they are forced to work in low paid jobs. The self-employed women workers are not able to increase the scope of their work due to this impediment. Thus, credit facilities at reasonable rates on regular basis through banks and government schemes should be provided to them so that they may improve their skills and enhance the scope of their jobs or works.
3. Women workers should make their livelihood need to produce regularly and sell and earn income at regularly intervals. There is need for adaptation to the changing trends, organized way of production and accurate costing. In other words the right combination of human, financial, physical and social capital is essential.

4. Uncertainty of work is the reason of dissatisfaction among the women workers. Lack of job security is the greatest problem of women workers that keep them confined to low wages, irregular and local employment. The fear of losing the job decreases their efficiency in work. Thus, steps should be taken by the government and the non-government organisations (NGOs) in this direction so that some sort of job security is provided to them. The NGOs should try to improve employer-employee relationship in the district.
5. There is no organization of women workers in the district. Thus, they have no bargaining capacity. The organization of women workers can help them in strengthening their position in employment. These organisations can enhance the scope of collective bargaining. The social organizations should help women workers in forming their organisations and developing leadership among them. The NGOs can help them by providing funds for their organisations.
6. The women workers who are living below the poverty line should be provided basic facilities such as food, clothes and housing or shelter at cheaper rates.
7. The government should specifically make policies and programmes to meet the needs of working women in unorganised sector. In policy-making bodies, these women should be given increased representation. It will help to improve the status of working women.
8. In addition to the above, a comprehensive review of the existing policies, programmes, schemes, legislation and social set up is needed so that women participation in work and at home is recognised. It is also essential to promote a new social attitude towards women workers. The key factors to achieve this objective are education and skill development training of the working women.
9. The media people should also be approached so that they cover the problems of working women in the district and

highlight them. More publicity should be made of the national laws to foster equal wages, better working conditions and more benefits for women workers in the unorganised sector.

10. To stop harassment and violence of women, broad-based campaigns are needed. Harassment of women on the way to work or at work should be publicized to promote action against it.
11. The domestic work should be recognised as a work, and they should be issued an Identity Card or/and letter of appointment.
12. Working hours for domestic workers should be fixed at 8 hours a day.
13. They should be paid overtime allowances in case they have to work longer.
14. They must be entitled to some personal free time during the day.
15. They must be entitled to a night's rest.
16. They must be entitled to one paid holiday in a week, and 15 days leave with wages after one year of service.
17. They should be allowed 15 days sick leave every year.
18. They should have access to the provisions of PF, and gratuity, and be provided with uniforms.
19. They should have living quarters which are strictly hygienic, and have security.
20. The employer should give one month's notice if he wants to dispense with the services of the worker.
21. There should be provisions in the law for periodic inspection to verify that the conditions in which domestic workers are employed are consistent with what the law lays down.

In the end it is suggested that concentrated and deliberate efforts should made by various agencies such as government, trade unions, employers' associations, NGOs etc. to improve the employment status of women workers in the district. These agencies should launch a joint programme to achieve the desired objectives. One of the reasons for the failure of this sector is gender inequality and lack of empowerment of women. There is a need to introspect the kind of programmes, including structural adjustment, which much of Africa was made to undergo in the past few decades, and the impact of such externally imposed policies on agriculture and much of the social sector.

I am of the firm opinion, that these measures will go a long way in improving the living and working conditions of the poor workers in the unorganised sector and inculcate in them the feeling of self-esteem, dignity and security.

"A nation would not march forward if women are left behind"— *Swami Vivekananda.*

Bibliography

Bibliography

Books and Journals

Acharya, Sarthi and A.V. Jose, "Employment and mobility: a study among workers of low-income households in Bombay city", (working paper), New Delhi: ILO-ARTEP, 1991.

Adams, J. and L. Paul, "The unorganised sector in India: work, gender and technology", in J.W. Bjorkman (ed.), The Changing Division of Labour in South Asia, New Delhi: Manohar Publications, 1987.

Aruee, G. and G. Mhone, "Employment promotion in the unorganised sector and the current economic crisis: the case of Southern Africa, ILO/SATEP, 1990.

Asian Productivity Organisation, "Strategies for developing the unorganised sector", Tokyo, 1995.

Aziz, Abdul, "Urban Poor and Unorganised Sector, New Delhi: Ashish Publications", 1984.

Anant, Suchitra, "Women and Work in India", Sage Publication, New Delhi, 1986.

Banerjee, Nirmala, "Women Worker in the Unorganized Sector", Sangam Books, Hyderabad, 1985.

Banerjee, Anita and Sen, Raj Kumar, "Women and Economic Development" (ed.), Deep and Deep Publications, New Delhi, 2000.

Bhoite, Anuradha, "Women Employees and Rural Development: Problems of Employed women in Rural Area", Gain Publishing House, New Delhi, 1987.

C.K. Hate, "Changing Status of Women", Allied Publications, Bombay, 1969.

Chadha G.K., "Unorganised sector in the Indian economy (paper presented at national workshop on strategic approaches to job creation in the urban unorganised sector in India), New Delhi: ILO, 2000.

Chandola, L.M., "Women in Unorganised Sector", Radiant

Publishers, New Delhi,1995.

Chowdhury Roy Supriya, Economic and Political Weekly, May 28-June 4, 2005, Nandal Santosh, "Women workers in unorganized sector: A study on construction industry in Haryana", International Journal of Development Issues, Year: 2006,Volume 5, Issue 2, pp. 119-132.

Commission of European Communities, International Monetary Fund, Organization for Economic Cooperation and Development, United Nations and World Bank (1993): System of National Accounts, 1993.

Central Statistical Organization, India (1998), National Industrial Classification.

Central Statistical Organization, India (2004), Report of the Working Group on Workforce Estimation for Compilation of National Accounts Statistics with base Year 1999-2000.

Central Statistical Organization, India (2006), Brochure on New Series of National Accounts Statistics, base year 1999-2000.

Datta, Ruddra, "Organising the Unorganised Workers" Vikas Publishing House, New Delhi, 1985.

David, Nancy, "Unorganised Women Workers: Problems and Prospect," Tripathi, S.N. (ed.) Unorganised Women Labour in India", Discovery Publishing House, New Delhi, 1996.

Desai, R.G., "Agricultural Economics", Himalaya Publishing House, Mumbai, 1998.

Davies, R., "The unorganised sector: a solution to unemployment", London: Catholic Institute for International Relations, 1978.

Everett, Jana and Mira Savara, "Organizations and unorganised sector women workers in Bombay", in Alice W. Clark (ed.), Gender and Political Economy: Explorations of South Asian Systems, Delhi: Oxford University Press, 1993.

Geertz, C., "Peddlers and princes: social change and economic modernization in two Indonesian towns", Chicago:

University of Chicago Press, 1963.

Ghosh, S. and A.K. Vohra, "Improvement of income and employment in the unorganised sector through enhancement of productivity with particular reference to the approach and structure adopted in India, in Strategies for developing the unorganised sector", Tokyo: Asian Productivity Organisation, 1995.

Gadgil, D.R., "Women in the working Force in India", Asia Publishing House, Mumbai, 1965.

Gajalakshmi, N., "Problems and Perspectives of Women Labour in India", Mohit Publication, New Delhi, 1996.

Giriappa, S., "The Role of Women in Rural Development", Daya Publishing House, Delhi, 1988.

Ganirade, K.D., "Women and Child Workers in Unorganised Sector", Concept Publishing Company, New Delhi, 1983.

Gowri, R Geetha, Reddy, P.J. and Rani, D. Usha, "Elderly Women: A Case Study of the Unorganized Sector", 2003, Eastern Book Corporation, Delhi.

Hussmanns, R., (1996), "ILO recommendations on methodologies concerning informal sector data collection" in Herman, B. and Staffers, W. (eds.): Unveiling the informal sector-More than counting heads (Aldershot/Brookfield/Hong Kong/Singapore/Sydney, Avebury), pp. 15-29.

Hussmanns, R., (1998), "Informal sector-statistical definition and survey methods", in Handbook of National Accounting, Household Accounting: Experiences in the Use of Concepts and Their Compilation, Volume 1: Household Sector Accounts, doc. ST/ESA/STAT/SERF/75, United Nations, New York, pp. 65-106.

Hussmanns, R., (1998), Developments in the design and implementation of informal sector and similar surveys-A review of national practices and experiences, Sixteenth International Conference of Labour Statisticians (Geneva, 6-15 October 1998), doc. ICLS/16/RD2, International

Labour Office, Geneva.

Hussmanns R., (2005), "Questionnaire on employment by selected characteristics.

International Labour Office, (1992), Fifteenth International Conference of Labour Statisticians (Geneva, 19-28 January 1993), Report III: Statistics of employment in the informal sector, doc. ICLS/1*5/111,* Geneva.

International Labour Office, (1993), Fifteenth International Conference of Labour Statisticians (Geneva, 19-28 January 1993), Report of the conference, doc. ICLS/15/D.6 (rev.l), Geneva.

ILO, "The urban unorganised sector in Asia: an annotated bibliography", International Labour Bibliography, No. 13., Geneva, 1992.

Jhabvala, Rehana, "The Unorganised Sector Work Security and Social Protection", Sage Publication, New Delhi, 2000.

Joshi, H., "The Unorganised Urban Economy and its Boundaries", Economic and Political Weekly, 15 (13): 1980: 638-644.

Kalpagam, U, "Labour and Gender Survival in Urban India", Sage Publication, New Delhi, 1994.

Lourdes, Beneria, "Women and Development: The Sexual Division of Labour in Rural Societies", Praeger Publications, New York, 1982.

Lubell, Harold, "The unorganised sector in the 1980s and 1990s. Paris: OECD, 1991.

Lund, F. and C. Skinner promoting the interests of women in the unorganised economy: an analysis of street trader organisations in South Africa. CSDS Research Report No. 19, Durban: University of Natal, 1999.

Mukhopadhyay, Swapna, "Role of the unorganised service sector in urban poverty alleviation in India, New York: UNESCAP, 1996.

Mazumdar, D., "The Rural-Urban Gap, Migration and the Working of Urban Labour Market: an Interpretation Based on a Study of the Workers of Bombay city", Indian Economic Review 18(2): 1983: 169-198.

Mead, D. and C. Morrison, "The Unorganised Sector Elephant", World Development, 24(1): 1996: 1611-1619.

Moser, C.O.N., "The Unorganised Sector Reworked: Viability and Vulnerability in Urban Development", Regional Development Dialogue, 5(2): Autumn 1984.

Mukhopadhyay, Swapna, "Locating Women Within Unorganised Sector Hierarchies", Indian Journal of Labour Economics 40 (3), July-September 1997: 483-92.

Manoria, C.B., "Agricultural Problems in India", Kitab Mahal, Allahabad, 1996.

Manohar, K.M. (ed.): "Socio-economic Status of Indian Women", Seema Publications, New Delhi, 1983.

Manohar and Shoba, V., "Maid Servants: Case Study Manohar", K.M. (ed.) Socio-economic Status of Indian Women", Seema Publications, New Delhi, 1983.

Mathur, R.N., "Quality of Working Life of Women Construction Workers", Commonwealth Publications, New Delhi, 1989.

Mukherjee, R.K., "Indian Working Class", Hind Kitab, Allahabad, 1991.

Margaret Hosmer Martens and Swasti Mitter, (eds.), Women in Trade Unions: Organizing the Unorganized, Geneva: International Labour Office, 1994.

Mitra, Arup (2001), "Employment in the Informal Sector" in Kundu, Amitabh and Alakh N. Sharma (ed.), Informal Sector in India-Perspectives and Policies, Institute for Human Development, New Delhi.

National Sample Survey Organisation, "Report Mo. 458 (Part I and Part II) on Employment and Unemployment Situation in India, 1999-2000".

Organization for Economic Co-operation and Development (2002), "Measuring the Non-Observed Economy-A Handbook".

Papa, Kondaveeti, "Women in Rural Areas", Chugh

Publications, Allahabad, 1982.

Papola, T.S., "Unorganised sector: concept and policy", Economic and Political Weekly, 15 (18): 3 May 1980: 817-824.

Papola, T.S., "Unorganised sector: concept and policy" in M.K. Rao, (ed.), Growth of Urban Unorganised Sector and Economic Development, Delhi, Kanishka Publications, 1994.

Papola, T.S., "Urban Informal Sector in a Developing Economy", Vikas Publishing House, New Delhi. 1981

Papola, T.S. and Sharma, Alakh, N., "Gender and Employment in India" (ed.), Indian Society of Labour Economics and Vikas Publishing House, New Delhi, 1999.

Panda, Damodar, "Labour in Unorganised Sector: The Devalued and the Deprived", Manak Publications, New Delhi, 1999.

Premi, M.K., "Migration to cities in India", in Rao, M.S.A. (ed.), Status in Migration, Manohar Publications, New Delhi,1986.

Rao, N.J.U., "Women in Developing Society", Ashish Publishing House, New Delhi, 1983.

Ronaldo Munck, The New International Labour Studies (London: Zed Books, 1988); Shauna L. Olney, Unions in a Changing World, Geneva: International Labour Office, 1996.

Rao, M.K., "The urban unorganised sector and urban development", in M.K. Rao (ed.), Growth of Urban Unorganised Sector and Economic Development, Delhi: Kanishka Publication, 1994.

Reveendran G. and Manna G.C. (2002), "Testing the conceptual framework of informal employment-A case study of India".

Santos, M., "The shared space: the two circuits of urban economy and their spatial repercussions", London: Methuen, 1975.

Sethuraman, S.V., "The urban unorganised sector in

developing countries", Geneva: ILO, 1981.

Shramshakti, "Report of the National Commission on Self-employed Women and Women in the Unorganised Sector", New Delhi: Ministry of Women and Child Welfare, 1988.

Singh, Surjit, "Some facets of unorganised sector in developing countries (mimeo)", Jaipur: IDS, 1994.

Soni Balbir, "Empowerment of Women Workers: The Unorganised Sector", Dominant Publishers and Distributors, New Delhi, 2007.

Singh, J.L. and Pandey R.K., "Women in Unorganised Sector: Problems and Prospects", Sunrise Publications, New Delhi, 2007.

Sundaram, S.K.G., "Emergence and development of unorganised sector in Mumbai", Paper presented at a seminar on Work and Workers in Mumbai-1930s to 1990s (mimeo), Mumbai: 27-29, November 1997.

Singh, D.P., "Women Workers in Unorganised Sector", Deep and Deep Publishers, New Delhi, 2005.

Shanti, K., "Issues Relating to Economic Migration of Females" in Sharma, A.N. and Singh, S. (ed.), Women and Work in India, B.R. Publishing Corporation, New Delhi.

Singla, A., "A study of work involvement of Agriculture women labourers in different activities", Manak Publications, New Delhi, 2000.

Sultanie, Madhu, "Women: Contract Labourers-A Deprivation Syndrome", Classic Publishing House, Jaipur, 1994.

Sundram, Satya I., "Plight of Unorganised women Workers", Tripathi, S.N. (ed.) Unorganised Labour in India, Discovery Publishing House, New Dehli, 1995.

Singh, J.L., Pandey, Ravi Kumar, Singh, Arun Kumar, "Women in Unorganised Sector: Problems and Prospects (ed.)", Sunrise Publications, Delhi, 2002.

Sengupta, Padmini, "Women Workers in India", Asia Publishing House Bombay, 1960.

Shankar, Guha Niyogi, "Beyond Conventional Trade Unionism in India," Bulletin of Concerned Asian Scholars 3, No. 24 (1992), Illina Sen, "Women's Participation in Trade Union Struggles," Economic and Political Weekly, 22, No. 27 (1987).

Sinha, Archana, "Social Security for Women in the Unorganised Sector: Human Development Perspective", April, 2008.

Sastry, N. S. (2004), "Estimating Informal Employment and Poverty in India", Discussion Paper Series-7, Human Development Resource Centre, UNDP, India.

Satpathy, Anoop (2004), "Size Composition and Characteristics of Informal Sector in India", NLI Research Studies Series No. 056/2004, V.V. Giri National Labour Institute, Noida.

Tripathi, S.N., Das Soudamini, "Informal Women Labour in India", Shing House, New Delhi, 1991.

Unni, Jeemol, "SEWA-NCAER project on contribution of the unorganised sector to national income, sector unit", Ahmedabad: SEWA, 1998.

Wishwakarma, R.K., "Unorganised sector linkages and its implications for development policy", in M.K. Rao (ed.), Growth of Urban Unorganised Sector and Economic Development, Delhi: Kanishka Publication, 1994.

Wishwakarma, R.K., "Urban unorganised sector: concept, policy issues and measures", Nagarlok, 12(1): 1980.

Saha, V., Kar A. and Baskaran T., "Contribution of Informal Sector and Informal Employment in Indian Economy (2004).

Articles

Agrawal, Bina: "Work Participation of Rural Women in Third World, Some Data and Conceptual Biases", Economic and Political Weekly December 21-28, 1985.

Anand, Vaijayanta: "Advocating for the Rights of Construction Workers: Nirman's Experience", The Indian

Journal of Social Work, Volume 59(3), July 1998.

Banerjee, N: "Trends in Women's Employment-1971-1981: Some Macro Observations", Economic and Political Weekly, April 29, 1989.

Bardhan, Pranab, K: "Labour Supply Functions in a Poor Agrarian Economy American Economic Review, Vol. 69, No. 1, 1979.

Bhalla, Sheila: "Workforce Restructuring, Wages and Want: Recent Events, Interpretations and Anaylsis", Indian Journal of Labour Economics, Vol. 39, No. 1, 1996.

Breman: "A Dualistic Labour System", Economic and Political Weekly, 1976.

Chadha, G.K: "Non-farm Employment for Rural Households in India: Indian Evidence and Progress," The Indian Journal of Labour Economics, 36(3), 1993.

Chakravarty, Shanti: "Women Power in Agriculture" Kurukehtra, November 16, 1975.

Chaudhuri, Satyabrata Rai: "Women's Place in the Labour Market", Indian, Express, May 13, 1995.

Chaudhary, Shama: "Mapping Women", Outlook, Vol. 10, 1999.

D'Souza, Ernol: "World Employment, ILO Perspective" Economic and Political Weekly, Vol. XXXIII, No. 39, 1998.

Fay, Weldone: "Women are Slaves but no Longer of Man", The Times of India, March 18, 1999.

Jain, D. and Srinivasan: "Women's Roles in Large Employment System", Ford Foundation Discussion Papers, No. 6, New Delhi, 1983.

Joshi, H: "Prospects and case of Employment of Women in Indian Cities", Economic and Political Weekly, 9(31-32 and 33) 1984.

Jumani, U: "Report of the National Workshop on Organising Self Employed women in India", Ahmedabad, 17-18, March, 1981.

Kalpagam, U: "Labour Market Segmentation in Multistructural Vol. 17, Context: Implications for India's Female Force", Labour, Capital And Society, Labour, No. 2, 1984.

Kalpagam, U: "Women work and Domestic Duties: Income Planning for Households", The Indian Journal of Labour Economics, Vol. 42, No. 4, 1979.

Kumari, Sudha: "Women workers in Unorganised Sector in India, Yojana, July 1-15, 1989.

Premi, M.K: "Aspects of Female Migration in India", Economic and Political Weekly, 15(15), 1980.

Singh, Hardayal: "Socio and Economic Condition of Agricultural Women Labours", Kurukshetra, September, pp. 10.

Singh, Gopal, Sharma, Prem S.R: "Structural Adjustment and Female Workers, Shyam Pand Bharadwaj, Mainstream" February 19, 1994.

Srinivasan, M.V: "Women workers in Unorganised Sector", Women's Link, 6(4) October-December, 2000.

Suryanarayan, S.S: "Information Base for the Informal Sector", Indian Journal of Labour Economics, Vol. 41 (3), July-September, 1998.

Shaizad, Sohail: "A study on Sexual harassment among working women", The Times of India, February 19, 1999.

Tagore, Ravindra Nath: "Women's Lot on East and West", Modern Review, November, 1912.

Unni, Jeemol: "Women in Informal Sector", Size Contribution to G.D.P., Gujarat Institute of Development Research, 1998, Ahmedabad.

Visaria, Pravin: "Women in the Indian Working Force", Anthavijuan, Vol. XXXIX, No. 1, March, 1997.

Wadhwa, Sonia: "Security Blankets for Women", Outlook, Vol. 8.

Index

Index